January 2018

Dear Sue, I hope you
enjoy my little book.
Love Bob

Common Sense Philosophy

Robert M. Craig, M.D.

YorkshirePublishing
www.yorkshirepublishing.com
Write Now.

Yorkshire Publishing
3207 South Norwood Avenue
Tulsa, Oklahoma 74135
www.YorkshirePublishing.com
918.394.2665

DEDICATION

To Joanne Craig, my wife of 50 years.

ACKNOWLEDGEMENTS

I am grateful for the helpful suggestions my friends; Les Hill, Bud Rice, John Clarke, Mark Dreyer, and Gail Bower; my brothers, Jon and Dick; and the rest of my family; gave in support of the essays. There was particular heated discussion of the essays on global warming and slavery, which induced a number of emendations.

CONTENTS

FORWARD

I call common-sense philosophy the investigation of important questions using our commonly used, everyday language and reasoning. This starting point appears to be incomplete, as it accepts reasoning firsthand, and what the reasoning process is, itself, is an important question. However, our common sense does not challenge whether or not we are able to reason. We are able to recognize when someone is unreasonable when they assert that they are unable to think reasonably. We use our reason to decide what is reasonable.

There are four important areas, or question fields, of common-sense philosophy, which are covered in this series of essays. These often overlap. The first concerns ourselves, our human nature. This is a component of the broader field, ontology, or being proper. The broader category is important in some philosophies or in metaphysical discourse, but it is only a small component of common-sense philosophy.

When we use our reason or our common sense we are looking into the question of truth. This broad philosophical discipline is called epistemology. How do we know something is true? Of course, this entails our reasoning capacity by which we judge the truthfulness of propositions. The ways in which we think or reason are the province of the second field of essays. We explore our nature to understand how we think or use reason to ascertain truth.

As we investigate our nature, we realize we are able to do things when we wish, and that we can give reasons for our actions. This is what we mean by free will. We also realize that there are marked inequalities among us. To various degrees, we have a sense that we ought to do something to rectify the inequalities, to improve the lives of others, often expressed in terms of fairness. This moral sense comes into conflict with our liberty or free will, as the expansion of equality for some restricts the liberty of others. The third set of essays deals with morality and how we ought to live.

The fourth group deals with the dynamic between liberty and morality in the polis: the political expression of our nature.

Common-sense philosophy has been elaborated throughout written history. Socrates used human examples to explore concepts of justice. Jesus' parables achieved similar effects. The Greco-Roman stoics, Epictetus and Marcus Aurelius, used commonplace examples in their teachings. Thomas Reid of the Scottish Enlightenment discussed the accession of knowledge by exploring how our sense organs work. The great 20th century Christian philosopher, C. S. Lewis, lectured in common-sense language. William James and the utilitarians, and the more modern analytic philosophers, employed similar procedures in their writing.

This philosophical volume contains some of the essays published in my first book, somewhat modified, in accordance with historical events over the past three years, but the essays' themes remain the same (1). They are included here as they complement the other essays in each of the four fields of discussion. They are also provided to those who have not obtained the first book.

Finally, I should note that I was a chemistry major in my undergraduate years at Colgate University, with a minor in philosophy. My career as a physician and research scientist, which began at Northwestern University, has influenced my thinking philosophically, and is rendered in some of the essays. Some of the discussions required modern scientific information, but I hope I explained things well enough for those who are not scientists. Some of my footnotes clarify the more difficult concepts, and references for further reading for the interested students are provided.

SECTION I. ONTOLOGY, BEING, HUMAN NATURE

This section deals with the general category, ontology, or being. From the standpoint of common-sense philosophy, it involves our being, or human nature. Essay 1, Human Nature, is a modification of the essay from my first philosophy book (1). Essay 2 discusses the characteristics of life itself, as we are examples of life as opposed to the physical world. The next two essays deal with the interaction between liberty and inequality, which are fundamental aspects of our nature: Essay 3, Slavery in the United States, and Essay 4, War. The latter is an update from my first book (1). The fifth essay, Shopping, deals with differences between our two sexes; the sixth, Free Will and the Physical World, expands the discussion of human nature in Essay 1.

Essay 1. Human Nature (1)

In many respects, the most important philosophical question is: what is human nature? How we live, including moral considerations, are dependent upon our nature. Epistemological questions cannot be asked without exploring our own reasoning capacity and our means of knowing. The ontological question of being itself is dependent upon our understanding of our own being. This essay will discuss the basic aspects of our human nature. It relies heavily on self-examination, but has been assisted by readings of others. I hope that most of the considerations will be obvious to each of us. The essay will not be extensively referenced; references will only be made as a part of general statements. Twelve categories will be discussed: consciousness of self; free action; consciousness of the world; biology; memory; responsibility; emotions; rational thought; moral thought and virtues; consciousness of time, gravity, space and causality; language and awareness of other people; and feelings of mystery and esthetic value. These aspects of our nature are not provable in the usual sense, as each of us experiences these features by means of our nature and expressed by our language. They are inferred and their verity is established by our own self-examination.

Self-Consciousness. Perhaps our earliest thought is self-consciousness. The agent involved in our action. The "I." The one engaged in judgment; the assimilator of experience; and the recipient of memory, dreams, and the spontaneous appearance of thoughts. It is unclear when self-consciousness is apparent as babies mature to childhood, and does not become apparent in others until language develops. Likewise, assessing whether lower animals have self-consciousness is difficult due to their lack of language and communication skills. One's consciousness of self develops with maturity and daily accretion of actions, experiences, memories, judgments, learning, emotions, and feelings.

Freedom. Along with our growing self-consciousness, our ability to act is apparent. This is realized first when we note our body and that we can freely use our body to do things. A baby can reach for a toy and can explore its characteristics. Early, we realize that we can cause things to ensue. Freedom of action becomes more apparent with maturity as actions are done for reasons, or justifications are made for the actions.

The World. Our ability to use our bodies to express our freedom includes our ability to apprehend that there is a world outside of our selves. The world is comprised of the physical universe that we are able to ascertain with our senses and manipulate with our bodies. As we apprehend the world, we realize that our sensory facilities complement one another, especially our senses of vision and touch; and, less so, smell, taste, position sense, and hearing. The three dimensional aspect of our world as partially conceived by our visual sensations is reinforced by our ability to feel the world and relate the visual input to three dimensions. Our common languages reinforce our understanding of the world.

Further, our bodies are part of the world, including our brains and nervous systems. The apparatus that allows us to discover the world is physical with its sensory and central nervous systems. The former provides the basic input and the latter the central processing machinery that allows for perceptions of the world and self-consciousness. There is a duality between the physical phenomena, the body and the peripheral and central nervous systems; and the mental consciousness and willful actions. The duality is evident by comparing the ability of one to perceive the world and to act within the world versus the physical mechanisms that occur alongside the mental images and actions.

The duality of the physical and the mental processes can be seen when our consciousness of the color red is compared to all of the events measurable in the physical world, paralleling the event. The description of the physical process, regardless of how exhaustive, including the complex optic nerves, and the neuronal activation in the occipital cortex, is not the same as the consciousness of red. Even though there are philosophic difficulties with the nexus between the two, it is clear that there is a duality.

Likewise, there are realities of our world that are not directly experienced, but are part of the fabric of experience, including space, time, causality, and gravity. These are basic to our world, induced from our everyday experiences, and cannot be proven or disproved. Although modern scientific concepts of space, time and gravity have evolved in cosmological and relativistic theories and are in contradistinction to our homely experiences, the presence of these four concepts in our common-sense world cannot be denied. The reality of our sensory apparatus is used in day-to-day language and is different from the reality described from scientific telescopes, spectroscopy, microscopy, nuclear accelerators, etc., and the resultant theorizing. Common sense, direct experience, elucidated in everyday language, is not less real than sophisticated scientific descriptions, which is expressed in its own language. Also, common sense is able to translate scientific theories into our everyday language.

Biology. As we explore the world and realize through personal experience and learning that our bodies are part of the world and are the vehicles through which we can accomplish things, we gradually become cognizant of other aspects of our biology. We learn that each of us is unique and that there are significant inequalities among us. Some are better endowed than others with those qualities that improve navigation through life. In a description of our nature it is important to realize that we are a biologic species, sharing many of the frailties of other species.

We have some features of plants and other animals. Among other animals, these include our respiratory, cardiovascular, digestive, excretory, locomotive, nervous, and reproductive systems. Most of these are involuntary. Some are unique or nearly unique to our species, such as our movable thumbs, our prodigious memories, our large cerebra, and our rich and complex emotions. There is a physical pleasure in realizing the normal physiologic processes of food ingestion, defecation, urination, sexual satisfaction, and increased cardiovascular activity with vigorous exercise. Conversely, disruption of these biologic activities produces painful signals to the brain: the discomfort of constipation, urinary retention, hunger, shortness of breath, chest pain, and sexual deprivation.

Additionally, there are biological, neural reactions in our brains that parallel these human functions, including our most complex actions of thinking and doing things for a reason.

We are an unequal species in many respects. Most of these inequalities are inherited, over which we have no control. Our endowments are mostly not our doing, whether salutary or not. Similarly, our cultural settings and biases are variegated.

Memory. There is a biologic, physical component to our memory, resembling in some respects the memory of computers. Unlike the computer memory, each of our own memories is unique. Memory is stored in our brains and can be brought to consciousness through electrical stimulation, either artificially by external electrodes or internally by neurogenic processes. Memory is comprised of all of our experiences: our previous actions and thoughts; our passions, hopes, dreams, and emotions; our learned behavior; and conceptions of our self and the world.

In many respects our memory is a clear reflection of who we are and is the content of our self-consciousness. Memory is an imprint of our self, as it contains the elements of our selfhood. It is not the same as our self, however, as we have the capacity as volitional actors to "bring up" memories, in much the same way that we can perform other actions. Memory can sometimes spontaneously enter our consciousness, with no volitional control; and memories can have some independent, neurological modifications, particularly evident in our dreams. In this respect memory is similar to sensory experience, as it enters our consciousness. Our dreams become conscious involuntarily in a similar way. Memory can sometimes be faulty, and sometimes can be refreshed by reminders. At times, effort impairs bringing up a memory, and a memory might "return" later, following an inability to bring up the memory at first. There are many involuntary characteristics of memory. In some respects, memory can be compared to our sensory and motor nervous systems in that it is under both voluntary control (our ability to act) and involuntary, reflex activity.

Responsibility. For free action, there is the necessary contingency that the actor is responsible for his action. Otherwise, there would be no difference between the physical world, which is governed by the laws of physics, and voluntary actions. A free action is performed for a reason or reasons, whereas events in the physical world are explained by causal connections. As noted above, causality is not directly observed. Rather it is inferred and is a part of our understanding. Scientific explanation hinges on acceptance of causality, even though it is not directly experienced. Human action done for a reason must be explainable by the actor in human language, not scientific language. Even though there are myriad physical events coinciding with the action, physical description does not describe the action, and has to be described in terms of common-sense, human reasons. The sense of the action is made by the human descriptions of the action. Regardless of the scientific depth of the event, it does not give an understanding of the action.

Responsibility parallels the amount of freedom exercised in the action. One clearly has no responsibility for his involuntary reflexes. Likewise, one does not have responsibility for his sentiments, feelings, desires, memories, and dreams that spontaneously appear in his consciousness, as he is not responsible for other passive sensory input. The more closely the event resembles passive human activity, the less responsible is the agent.

Emotions. Needs, wants, empathy, pride, sympathy, envy, anger, grief, shame, guilt, love, and other feelings are also part of our nature, although experienced differently in each of us. They are clearly our own, although they can be shared with other people. They provide some of our reasons for our actions. For example, our need for survival can influence activity involved in satisfying that need, such as obtaining gainful employment. The experience of these emotions can be ennobling and can spur dignified actions. It can also induce ignominious actions. We have little control or responsibility over these emotional experiences, as they spontaneously appear in our consciousness. Our responsibility resides in what we do about them: how we act.

Rational Thought. It is impossible to argue that we act reasonably or rationally using our reason. Our reason is basic to our nature and is the facility we use to assert or argue that propositions are reasonable. We cannot use reason to prove reason. Rather, reason is used to investigate all other questions and statements. Conclusions derived from reason are of three types. The first is deductive, necessarily true assuming the basic axiomatic structure is true. This is the reasoning employed by mathematical systems. For example, in Euclidean geometry, parallel lines never meet. This is necessarily true and is tautological within the Euclidean system. In other, non-Euclidean, systems, such as spherical geometry, the statement is not always true. Systems of logic are extensions of these tautological truths. We use logic or reasoning to prove or disprove statements, which may be fallacious or illogical.

On the other hand, truth or falsity of statements about the world are not necessarily true and can be disproved by one example found in the world that contradicts the statement. The truth of the statements is contingent upon empirical evidence. In brief, this is the major process involved in advancing scientific theories. Theories cannot be true of the world if one example of their falsity is shown. The theory then has to be modified or abandoned. Similar to the development of scientific theories, some of our basic concepts of causality are induced from the regularity of experience, as causality itself is not experienced. These induced concepts are contained within our everyday language and scientific theories.

The third variety of reasoning is employed in our common-sense, daily interactions. For example, there are statements that are unreasonable through mistaken use of language. It is clearly fallacious for someone to assert that my claim that I am feeling pain is untrue. I am the only one who can make that claim. Others can indicate that the pain is "not real" in the usual sense, but that the pain is an hallucination. Clarification of the statement by further explanation makes sense of the statement, showing that both statements can be true, as they state different things. The clarifying statement can be supported through other evidence, such as the patient's long-term problem with schizophrenia, hallucinations, and delusions. However, no amount of clarification can eliminate the reality that the subject is experiencing pain. Only the subject can make that statement. We use all of these reasoning facilities – deduction, induction, and language clarification – in our daily lives.

The reasoning capacity requires teaching and learning as one journeys through childhood. Although the ability to reason is innate or a part of our nature, its use is cultivated through education, especially by parents, other members of one's family, and teachers. As exemplified by the individual with pain, the facts of the situation can be clarified by the modulating effect of the reasoning process of other people.

Morality. An ethical sense is a component of our nature too. It does not make sense to use reason to prove that reason is reasonable. We use reason to show that propositions are reasonable or unreasonable. Similarly, we use our moral sense to show whether an action is morally sound or not. There would be no ground for making a moral or normative judgment if we did not share a moral sense. This is not to say that we will have agreement among ourselves regarding the morality of a specific action. On the contrary, morality is complex and nuanced. There are multiple countervailing points of view that come to play in making moral judgments. There are exceptions to all moral dicta. For example, one ought not to kill; yet killing may be acceptable if a rapist is threatening your child's life with a knife. This is not to say that morality is always "relative," implying that there is nothing "absolute" with morality. It is to say that moral questions are complex and often require careful consideration using our moral nature. This sense is expressed in our feelings of empathy and sympathy for others undergoing suffering. It is also seen in our desire to bring about some equality for those less fortunate, the provision of charity in our human interactions, and our political institutions, which foster equality at the expense of individual liberties. Finally, from a negative standpoint, we experience shame and guilt when we act immorally, although these emotions are not uniformly felt.

From a larger perspective, our moral sense provides a structure upon which our life decisions should be made. Humans are ennobled when their behavior is virtuous, although conflicts among the virtues may come into play. For example, courage is a virtue, but prudence can also be a virtue. Likewise, pride in one's work and its resultant self-esteem are virtuous, but can be modified by humility and charity. We use our moral sense in adjudicating behavior among life's contingencies and virtuous standards.

Thinking and morality go hand-in-hand. Each is a component of our nature and each matures into adulthood. The process of thinking is developmental. An embryo implanted in a woman's uterus has all of the potential of a thinking being, but the reasoning function is acquired incrementally, coming to fruition during childhood, coincident with the use of language. Although the ability to think is innate, it needs to be fostered.

Likewise, the ability to make moral judgments is innate, a component of our nature. It also needs to be nurtured. In many respects the Aristotelian concept of the moral individual's being habitually moral through developed habit describes his moral makeup. A person takes on characteristic behavior that is expected during moral challenges.

His moral behavior becomes a component of his self-hood. A public persona becomes evident, although it is never completely public, as the motivation or reasons for actions are not always known and may be incorrect. In spite of his reputation, Iago was not an honest, honorable man. The usual, moral behavior of someone should not be interpreted as a cause of his behavior, as one can always do otherwise. A better description is a patterned behavior that describes who he is.

Time, Space, Gravity, Causality. Coincident with our realization that there is an outside world, our physical bodies are a component of the world, and we can freely act in the world simply by doing; there is the evolving realization of time, space, gravity and causality. We don't experience them directly; rather they are acquired realizations that we induce, and they are the fabric of our existence. As we learn to move about in the world, we have to contend with gravity, and it is always with us. Likewise, space is the environment of things, our world. We experience the individual things but space itself is inferred.

Recent scientific and mathematical investigations of the atomic world have shown quite convincingly that descriptions at the subatomic level are only possible statistically. The velocity and momentum of elementary particles cannot be described simultaneously. In addition, the location of an elementary particle is best characterized as a statistical cloud. Further, electromagnetic waves have both particulate and wave-like features. Although these theories are disturbing to our common-sense concepts of causality, they do not disrupt our scientific understanding of the macro-world, the world in which we live, which is described in terms of our classic views of causality, both from scientific and common-sense standpoints. In aggregate, our world behaves causally, even though there is unpredictability of the behavior of elemental particles in the micro-sphere. The scientific description of quantum mechanics does not disrupt the above depiction of the evident duality of events in the physical world and actions done for a reason. The former relies on statistical or causal explanations. The latter uses human language, which provides homely reasons for actions.

Similarly, the persistent ticking of the time clock is always present. We experience time in four ways. First are the infinitesimal units of time, described by differential calculus in terms of infinite limits. Time is conceptualized mathematically as a continuous function rather than as a discontinuous one. From this standpoint, velocity is described by the change of distance over the change in time, as the change in time approaches its limit of zero, which is an infinite regression.

However, we cannot experience an infinitely small duration. Rather, we have a sense of the march of time in small units, comprised like frames of a movie. But, we experience the flow of time like the movie itself. These are the longer stretches of time, which we experience holistically and not in small units. Some have called this a stream of consciousness, which is a good description. It is the stream of consciousness that is incorporated in our memory and becomes a component of us (2). The physicochemical biology of retained memory is in chunks like computer bytes. Our conscious perception of memory is entirely different and is described in common-sense, not scientific, language. On the other hand, our memory stores and retrieves things as compilations of individual events although each physical element is stored separately. The physical element is like the frame in a movie, but the retrieved event is the movie itself.

Thirdly, time is experienced relativistically in modern scientific theories that try to explain phenomena cosmologically or events occurring at velocities close to the speed of light (3). Time is considered a dimension, similar to length, width and height. None of the four dimensions is absolute and they vary dependent upon the closeness to the speed of light. These concepts are foreign to our natural experiences of time, as the velocities on Earth are slow in comparison to light's. Our common-sense experiences of time better reflect our nature.

A fourth consideration is the very personal realization that our time is limited. Each day may be our last. Tomorrow, our loved ones might be murdered. Our very being is enmeshed in its limited duration. Much of literature, religious exercises, poetry, and philosophy deal with this basic fact of our nature. Our day-to-day dealing with our health, death, and fate are manifestations of the limited time we have in this world.

It is difficult to conceive of a world without gravity, time, and space. Looked at cosmologically, space, time, and the things of the world were presumably produced by the "big bang," with the expansion of space and time, expressed in increasing entropy, and eventuating in gravity, which is the architecture of space.

Other People; Language. The most obvious example of our being social creatures is in the use of our language. Language can only be understood in terms of other people. There are unspoken, non-verbal communications learned and practiced by infants (grimacing, smiling, crying, laughter, arm movements, etc.), and these are translated into language by convention. Naming things is also derived from this use of conventions. Language is organic and is constantly evolving. The structure of language is complex and can bring about misinterpretations and fallacies, usually clarified by massaging and elucidating statements and, sometimes, by enlisting a referee. For example, two people might have a dispute over a proposition, but the involvement of another person or a dictionary resolves the issue. Language disputes are often settled in this way.

Our reasoning processes are couched in specific language systems, none of which is all-inclusive. An axiomatic system for arithmetic can be internally consistent, yet can be shown to be incomplete in that very logical system, as demonstrated by Gödel's Proof (4).

The language of the scientific description of the micro-world of elementary particles must rely on statistical descriptions, which are anathema to the usual descriptions of common-sense experience or the causal descriptions of the macro-world (3). In a sense, a translation is required for the descriptions provided by quantum mechanical theories of the atomic and subatomic world into our macroscopic experience of everyday life. Strange concepts of superposition of subatomic particles, described by equations involving imaginary numbers (numbers that contain the square root of -1, designated by i) need to be used to describe this micro-world, and need not contradict our understanding of the macroscopic world, which is the agglomeration of these tiny particles (3).

Finally, the language of science is that of the brain, whereas the language of poetry and song is from the heart. No scientific explanation can describe the emotional experience of listening to the love duet from La Boheme better than poetry.

Mystery. The ancients staring at the night-time sky, the astronomers astounded by the vastness of the universe and the wonders of cosmology, the physicists exploring the intricacies of subatomic particles and the limitations of our knowledge and understanding, the poets' awful task of explaining the profundity of love, the joy in listening to the triumphal Beethoven's Ninth Symphony, the intricate beauty of the eye, and the ineffable feeling we have surrounding our finitude and eventual death into eternity all show our aesthetic or spiritual nature. The awe endures. This aspect of our nature is perhaps the most ennobling: our impotence over the loss of our loved one, shaking our fist at the gods and our humble, selfless, prayerful thanks to mysteries we do not understand.

CONCLUSION

These twelve aspects of our nature are the bases for exploring the other important philosophical issues, including how we live; how we know and whether we can grasp truth; and being itself, in an ontological sense. How we live should be consistent with our nature. Moral or normative discussions would be fruitless if we did not have a natural, moral sense, upon which reasonable discourse would ensue. The epistemic questions are dependent upon how we reason and what is reasonable. If reason were not part of our nature, searching for truth would make no sense. Our ontological understanding of being is dependent upon our understanding of our own being. Many of the ultimate questions that we ask regarding our own mortality and existence itself rest upon our understanding of our own nature. These essential features of our nature cannot be deduced, as they are the central bases of what we are. They can be inferred and described through our self-exploration and become the strata for reasonable discourse about the world and us.

Essay 2. Unique and Universal Characteristics of Life

Background

Life is the most prominent feature of Earth, perhaps starting four billion years ago in our oceans as unicellular, prokaryotic, organisms, called Archaea, which lived in a world devoid of oxygen. About 2.5 billion years ago, life underwent drastic changes initiated by the appearance of mono-cellular plants possessing chloroplasts. These permitted photosynthesis, converting water and carbon dioxide into energy-rich organic compounds and oxygen. This fostered the animal kingdom, which consumed the organic chemicals through oxygenation (respiration), releasing carbon dioxide and reinforcing the green plant/animal cycle.

Life is resilient and difficult to eradicate, having survived many cataclysmic events and massive extinctions, induced by volcanic eruptions or meteor impactions (5). It is found almost everywhere, in the depths of the ocean, Polar Regions, deserts and mountaintops.

Life is characterized by many faculties including reproduction, respiration (oxidation of organic or inorganic chemicals), incorporation of raw materials into biologic chemicals, and excretion of waste products. Among these, is there one that describes life and distinguishes it from other components of the universe? A definition of life, separate from the non-vital world is elusive.

The attempt to understand the nature of life is an ontological, philosophical undertaking. What is (are) the essential characteristic (s) of life, found in all living things and absent from the non-living? What is the nature or fundamental being of life?

Are Homo Sapiens a Distinct Species?

One approach to this problem is to investigate ourselves, identifying one feature that describes us uniquely from other forms of life. This process could be used as a model to investigate life.

Since humans are phylogenetically more advanced than other species, it is reasonable to consider our more complex characteristics as measures of our individuality. Humans are warm-blooded, multicellular organisms (eukaryotes). We can move and have sophisticated muscular, neurological and structural systems, similar to other mammals. Humans also have complex defense mechanisms, including immunologic and hematological abilities, a circulatory system that distributes products throughout the body, and specific mechanisms to control temperature, depending upon environmental challenges. We also think; have self-awareness; possess a moral sense; communicate with others through language; and have memories and feelings, mostly out of our control. There are both uncontrollable, reflex components of our behavior; and actions that are performed for reasons, enunciated in our language. All of these mental facilities have a parallel physical nervous system, which is partially under our control and partially controls our physical activities.

Which of these advanced features is unique to our species, not shared by others? In addition, which is universally present among those of our species? Phylogenetically, our closest ancestors – the chimpanzees, bonobos, and apes – also possess these complex systems.

How do we identify ourselves? Are the bacteria on our skin and in our digestive tract part of us? More bacteria cells are contained within us than our classically defined, corporal cells. Bacteria provide benefits through nutrient digestion and immunologic activity against pathogens. These bacteria could be considered one of five gradations of our being. Our selves are, first, our conscious selves, the "I" of our interactions, the communicator who uses language, the agent freely and responsibly performing actions for reasons. A second tier is our memory. A third is the physicochemical activity that parallels our consciousness and allows for our memory and our actions. A fourth is our physical body with all of its complexity. Finally, the fifth tier is comprised of the living beings on our skin and digestive tract, and, perhaps, in our excrement.

Tier 1 alone is unique and universally present among us. The distinguishing characteristic of Homo sapiens is individual consciousness: the ability to reason, think morally, act freely and responsibly, self-reflect, and use language to explain one's individual mental state to others. Although other animals have rudimentary language facilities and some feelings of empathy, only humans have the full panoply of consciousness, freedom, and a moral sense.

Of these, free will and responsibility are the most clearly distinguishing features. We cannot get inside the mind of a chimpanzee and ask it whether it has a concept of self. Free will and responsibility require our being able to express our reasons for our actions within the human stage, and to embrace the responsibility for the actions. If a chimpanzee were to develop the facilities of free action, it would be human, and self-consciousness, language, reasoning, and a moral sense would accompany their acquisition. Conversely, the loss of free will and responsibility makes one no longer fully human (for example through severe brain injury).

Unique Feature of Life

Turning to life, we can use this approach to define those things that are universally present for all life entities, and distinguish them from other things in the universe, the non-living. Our method involving humans looked for a feature or features that are found exclusively in humans and exist in all humans. Human consciousness, especially free will and responsibility, fulfilled that mission.

In contrast, characterizing life must consider the phylogenetically early forms: the unicellular prokaryotes rather than the multicellular organisms, as the latter contain all the features of the former. These facilities are reproduction, respiration, incorporation and processing of raw materials, excretion of waste products, and at least one living cell containing these functions.

Among these, an obvious candidate for defining life might be reproductive activities aligned with species survival. This appears to be universally present among all life forms, although the individual processes show a host of differences among species. Along this line, one could nominate chains of nucleic acids (RNA or DNA). For example, DNA is fundamental to reproduction and genetics for higher animal forms, but many unicellular organisms, particularly viruses, possess RNA as the basic reproductive chemical. Also, the nucleic acids require other chemicals, including protein enzymes which catalyze their reactions. Further, there are different strategies involved in species preservation. Higher multicellular organisms employ sexual reproduction. Archaea and bacteria utilize direct transfer of genetic material between species and self-duplication by binary fission. Many plants employ budding of spores as their primary reproductive strategy. These variations show that there is no universally defining element. Finally, the molecular processes involved are similar to the basic chemistry seen in non-living chemical reactions, adhering to the same laws.

Survival itself is not unique to biology, as many chemical phenomena have a tendency to preserve their integrity. For example, crystals continue to form and maintain their existence, so long as the environment remains permissive.

Some of the biologic, chemical processes are universally present in all life. Respiration, oxidation of organic or inorganic chemicals, is required for life as it is responsible for the energy generation for all of life's processes. Some of the earliest living entities, Archaea, present in our oceans prior to the development of photosynthesis and the oxygenation of our atmosphere and oceans, possessed the ability to oxidize bivalent to trivalent iron utilizing the ocean's iron-sulfur rich milieu (6), possibly in the walls of alkaline, inorganic vents (7). This primitive oxidation was analogous to the respiration involving oxygen in more phylogenetically advanced species. However, oxidation is not unique to biology, as it is evident prominently in the inorganic world.

Recent research supports the involvement of quantum mechanics in some of life's processes, quantum biology. For example, photosynthesis relies on a strategy involving the probabilistic nature of subatomic particles, such as electrons, that permit reactions to ensue across major energy gradients. The "activated" electron has a statistical probability to "be" in multiple locations simultaneously, until it is "measured" or located in its new location (8).

Simply stated, photosynthesis harnesses the energy from the sun by "oxidizing water," providing an energized electron that is transported along an "electron train," which is an energy source that is eventually stored within ATP (adenosine triphosphate), the predominant cellular energy source. The energized electron is eventually donated to the carbon atom in CO_2 ("reducing" it), producing hydrocarbons and molecular oxygen. The remarkable chloroplasts which house the photosynthetic process receive energy from the sun, producing energy-rich ATP, which provide the energy for the cell. Photosynthesis also produces the energy-rich carbohydrates which are used by animals for energy generation via respiration with the oxygen produced by green plants. The cycle is completed by animals generating CO_2 for photosynthesis (9).

Quantum biology is also entailed in the kinetics of involved enzymes. Chemical reactions proceed through intermediate states that are at higher energy levels than the original and eventual components. Energy needs to be used for classical chemical reactions to ensue. Catalysts can also facilitate the process. Enzymes are biologic catalysts, comprised of proteins, strings of amino acids. These enzymes promote photosynthesis throughout their activation process, bringing the reaction products close enough for the reactions to ensue. There is recent evidence that quantum mechanisms are also involved. The activated electron displays wave behavior, allowing it to settle in its eventual location (on another molecule) (8). In a sense, the wave function allows for a "tunneling" through the energy barrier and the electron's eventual residing in its new locus (10).

Although quantum biology describes photosynthesis and other biologic processes, quantum mechanics cannot claim a special existence in biology, as it also describes inorganic chemical reactions. Further, physical processes such as nuclear fusion within our sun require a similar "tunneling" of two hydrogen atoms, eventuating in helium and overcoming the repulsive energy between the two positively charged hydrogen nuclei. Although quantum biology is essential for life, the quantum wave function is not unique to life, being present in all matter.

Enzymes are also essential for life, present in all life forms. They catalyze most vital functions. Although they are present in all biology, they are not unique to biology. The constituent protein chains can be synthesized in the laboratory and are not living by themselves. Presumably, before life began, there were peptide chains (early proteins) among other essential chemicals that were not alive. Proteins within living cells require finely tuned reactions involving genetic DNA, which delivers formulas to RNA molecules that orchestrate protein synthesis within a reticular framework involving the constituent amino acids, delivered by organelles called ribosomes (11).

Likewise, nucleotide chains (RNA and DNA) are essential for life, but can be synthesized in the laboratory and are not living. Further, there are life forms, such as RNA viruses, that do not contain DNA. Finally, nucleotides present in the primordial soup or in protocells in the alkaline vents in early oceans prior to the onset of life were not alive (7). Proteins, enzymes, and nucleotides are necessary for life, but each is not sufficient. Each moiety is dependent upon the other constituents.

These chemical components of life need to be compartmentalized along with inorganic chemicals in a cell for life to exist. All of life is comprised of cells. Living cells are the characteristic entities that are both unique to life and universally present among all of life's entities. The identity of an individual cell is assured by a membrane that separates it from the outside world. These cell membranes are necessary for life but are not sufficient by themselves for all of life's processes, as they require proteins and nucleic acids for their synthesis. The cell is the locus where these organelles perform in beautiful harmony. It allows for respiration, reproduction, photosynthesis, intracellular transport, ingress of nutrients and egress of waste.

Some organelles of cells may be primitive life forms that have been incorporated in the cell: mitochondria, ribosomes, and cell nuclei. Other primitive life entities are parasitic, including viruses, which require the host DNA for replication.

Living things are either unicellular, in the case of prokaryotes (Archaea and bacteria) and viruses, or multicellular (eukaryotes). Their cells are complex with sophisticated membranes that allow for active and passive ingress of nutrients, water and electrolytes; and egress of waste products, electrolytes and water. Their intracellular organelles allow the orderly processing in protein synthesis (chromosomes or DNA; ribosomes, containing RNA; and structural, reticular membranes).

Many of these proteins are enzymes that catalyze the critical, chemical, intracellular reactions. Each cell has genetic or hereditary schemes. There are also mechanisms for intracellular trafficking of their various constituents. Finally, each has the ability to oxidize fuels, which produces energy. All of these functions are essential for life. The living cell contains them all.

CONCLUSION

Defining the essential and universal nature of life and human consciousness from the remaining observable world is an ontological problem, which explores the nature or being of these three spheres. Although this essay was grounded on scientific material, it is essentially a philosophical essay. The material world, life, and human consciousness are the three entities of the world and have different natures.

In defining the unique nature of life, it was useful to describe the essential characteristic of human life. Human consciousness, embodying freedom, responsibility, and a moral sense, are unique to humans and are shared by all humans. Similarly, life is characterized by the living cell, which shares all of the features of living things, distinct from the rest of the universe and is present in all of life.

Essay 3. Slavery in the USA

Introduction

Jefferson's lofty Declaration of Independence, and the eventual Constitution of the United States of America contain some of the most brilliant political expressions ever uttered. God-given or natural rights and liberties are enunciated. Equality is promulgated, although not as vehemently as are individual liberties. In spite of this praiseworthy beginning, the new Union proceeded to foster slavery of black Africans and their progeny; to eliminate, nearly completely, Native Americans; to wage war against its southern neighbor, Mexico, in its quest for territorial expansion; to undergo one of the most bloody civil wars in history over the expansion of slavery; and to continue many of the elements of slavery to African-Americans, in spite of slavery's elimination. This essay is an attempt to explore, and, perhaps, to explain this disparity between the ideals expressed and the eventualities. It will be argued that slavery is a consequence of human liberty and that its elimination is due to political enactment in our quest for some equality. Liberty and equality are in opposition in this dynamic.

First, this exposition explores our human nature, especially our free will on the one hand and the promotion of equality on the other. Navigating these opposing aspects of our nature is one of the most profound features of our humanity. War and slavery are shown as political developments of unhindered liberty. Slavery is present throughout human history. War has often been an accompaniment.

Slavery's eventual elimination or amelioration from some modern societies is then discussed. These salutary developments relate to our natural tendency, as individuals and political entities, to advance equality, as expressed by the Founding Fathers, coordinated with successful developments within these political entities. Further, other outgrowths of this expansion have occurred for all humans, regardless of their race, gender, political views, religion, or sexual orientation. Finally, cautious words conclude that our human capacity to overwhelm our moral nature by undue expansion of some of the more unsavory aspects of our liberty may occur. The horrors of the twentieth century and its two world wars confirm this possibility.

Human Nature, Reason, Free Will, Inequality, Morality

To understand our nature, introspection and observation of ourselves in action are required. It is difficult to prove objectively our nature using our nature, as our characteristics are involved in the process. For example, we are able to think rationally, to reason, to deduce, and to make inferences, which are features of our cognitive nature. We use reason to judge the truthfulness or soundness of propositions. Yet, it is impossible to prove reason using our reason. The ability to use reason is already incorporated. Our reasoning capacity is a starting point for sensible discussion.

Similarly, there are other features of our nature that are clearly present but difficult to prove in the usual sense. Our free will is evident by exploring the distinction between causal events and freely performed human actions. The world is generally perceived to behave causally, as events show connectivity, which allows us to infer causality. Although the causal nexus is not observed in itself, it is induced and makes sense of or clarifies our world. Most scientific observations are based upon this causal inference. Our world behaves causally, even though the causal connections themselves are not observed.

On the other hand, human actions done for or justified by reasons are the hallmarks of our free will. The clarification of actions is generally given in common-sense, conversational language. There are two simultaneously related events. The first is the occurrence on the human stage, requiring a subjective explanation, the reason for an action, known fully only by the individual actor. The second event is the entire causal network accompanying the action, potentially described completely by an outside observer.

The distinction between the two events can be clarified by an example. A pitcher throws a curve ball to the inside corner of the leadoff batter for the opposing team, which the batter misses wildly. The pitcher explains his action, "I threw the curve ball as I knew the batter was a sucker for that pitch." The common-sense description of the event is somewhat complicated as it also includes knowledge of the game, including its language and intricacies: curve ball, pitch, pitcher, batter, sucker, etc. Clearly understood, however, is the fact that the pitcher freely performed the action and was responsible for it. Looked at from a causal standpoint, there were a host of occurrences, including the musculoskeletal actions of the pitcher, his neurological and biochemical changes within the peripheral and sensory nervous systems, the speed and direction of the baseball, etc. Regardless of how complex the physical explanation is, it is entirely different from the pitcher's. The dualism of the two events is obvious. Freedom and responsibility, then, are features of our being, perhaps our most characteristic ones. Our liberty allows us to function in the world, satisfying our basic and secondary needs.

A third, natural reality is our inequality. Each of us is unique, with obvious differences, including body habitus, intelligence, ethnic and parental backgrounds, biases, intrinsic abilities, and indigenous culture. A fourth aspect is our moral or ethical sense, which comes into play when liberty is expanded for one group at the expense of another's, usually to provide some equality. Political processes are generally mediated along these lines, producing fairness while diminishing liberties of some in the process. Liberty and equality can be viewed politically in counterposition.

Slavery as Unrestricted Liberty

Slavery is an unbridled, tyrannical expression of liberty for one group over another. War is likewise a development of unhindered freedom. The relationship between war and slavery is evident throughout history. Roman triumphs were attended by displays of slaves from conquered territories. Prior to the Islamic expansions beginning in the ninth century, slavery was mostly practiced between clans or tribes, so-called kinship-produced slavery, with capture of slaves from enemies during warfare (12). Slavery expanded greatly during the period of Islamic hegemony over the Middle East, Northern Africa, and parts of the Mediterranean Basin, from the ninth to nineteenth century. It has been estimated that the volume of the Islamic slave exports from Africa to the Islamic regions was in the range of 10 million and the number of killed or retained as slaves in Africa was at least 10 million (12). The European-African transatlantic connection expanded slavery further with estimates of 15 million slaves transported in this process from the seventeenth to the nineteenth century (12).

The slavery industry was transformed considerably with the transatlantic passage. All European nations took part in this activity, although some to a much larger degree. The four centuries of the transatlantic slave passage may have equaled or superseded the volume of intra-African and Islamic slave trade (12).

There were major distinctions between the transatlantic and other slavery entities. First, slaves transported to the new world were seen as foreign, arising from distant lands, with different skin pigment and racial characteristics from the Europeans'. Secondly, the slaves did not become assimilated into the culture of the new world, as they did in Africa, the Mideast, and the Indian subcontinent. Further, unlike the Islamic slaves, the children of the slaves were not emancipated from slavery. Finally, the Islamic and intra-African slavery practices favored women and children for domestic or sexual reasons, whereas the transatlantic variety, especially in its earlier stages, favored young men or boys who could function as labor (12).

Prior to the nineteenth century, slavery was accepted in Europe, incorporated in its political and economic systems. Serfdom was similar to slavery, although not as extreme. Most Europeans accepted the notion that black Africans were subhuman, giving the institution of African slavery some legitimacy, although obviously erroneously. The worldview of the white, propertied, male European was his preeminence over women, other races, minors, and men with no property. The Europeans who explored and developed the New World mostly shared this mindset.

On the other hand, the pronouncements of the Founding Fathers regarding liberty and equality were revolutionary. It is difficult to affirm how strongly the views were held when considering the fate of black African slaves, who comprised 20% of the new Republic's population (12).

At the time of the drafting of the Declaration of Independence and the United States Constitution, and the American Revolution, much of the Union's power rested in the southern states. This is manifested by the fact that most of the presidents prior to the Civil War originated from the South. In addition, four of the first five presidents were slaveholders from Virginia, including our most liberal, Thomas Jefferson.

Major constitutional compromises were deemed necessary to preserve the fledgling republic, including the 3/5 proportional census ruling on slaves, determining the makeup of the House of Representatives and the Electoral College, and the failure constitutionally to emancipate slaves. The Constitution did include the provision that the new republic would disallow the transatlantic passage of slaves after 1807, although children born of slaves would remain property of the slave owners.

So the disparity between the sentiments expressed in the documents drafted by the Founding Fathers and the eventual, continued expansion of slavery is partially explained by the European view that black Africans were subhuman, and that maintaining slavery was necessary to preserve the fragile union of the original thirteen states. Multiple compromises were required to establish the union of North and South.

There were two other important factors involved. First was the importance of the slave industry's support of the burgeoning capitalist system. Second was the requirement to prevent the hegemonic pretensions of the European nations: Spain, England, and France (13).

Perhaps Thomas Jefferson was the most progressive or liberal of the Founding Fathers. His enunciations of liberty and equality for all in the Declaration of Independence are peerless. In spite of this, he was flawed. Not only did he own slaves, he took on one of his slaves as a mistress, with whom he fathered children. His actions exemplify the depth of the incorporation of black African slavery in the southern American consciousness. Exploitation of one's property, a female slave, was considered acceptable behavior.

As our third president, he had to navigate difficult political issues in the quest to preserve the Union. Prominent in these considerations was its economic development. Slavery was a critical component of the nation's early capitalism and its place in the world economy. Its effects were not isolated to the South. Rather, they were elements of the worldwide economy of the industrial revolution, especially the textile industry (13). Slavery provided a cheap labor source for cotton farming. The cotton was the raw material for the textile factories of England, and, later, of the northern states. Financing the South was provided through the purchase of cotton and through banks providing credit to the plantations for purchasing slaves and the further development of plantations. Interdependence of the southern plantations, the labor of slavery, cotton, credit from banks, the textile industry, and the transatlantic slavery passage were reinforced. Slavery's expansion continued with the children of slaves, following the discontinuance of the transatlantic passage. Both the North and the South felt that the preservation of slavery and its expansion were necessary for the economic success of the new Union. Emancipation of slaves was unpopular in both the North and South.

In addition to slavery's critical importance in supporting the capitalism of the United States, it was also used in the development of the West beyond the Appalachians, to Tennessee, Kentucky, western Georgia, Alabama, Mississippi, and Louisiana. The European nations, England, France, and Spain, had an interest in this area, particularly New Orleans and the Mississippi River.

The political advantage of the Union's expansion was to promote its claim to these areas. European interests waned with the diminution of Spanish power and the fall of the French, Napoleonic Empire. The expansionist claims of the new Republic and its exclusive rights were enhanced further by the Louisiana Purchase from France, the purchase of Florida from Spain, the war of 1812, and the Monroe Doctrine.

Slavery's expansion into the new territories was assisted by the access to easy credit for the purchase of land and slaves. In addition, the Federal Government promoted the Indian wars against the Seminoles in Florida; and the Creek, Cherokee, and Chickasaw nations in the newly formed southern territories. Eventually the Native Americans were largely killed or displaced from these territories.

The general acceptance of the expansion of the United States was similar to the colonial enterprises of European nations: Portugal, Spain, Holland, England, France, and Germany. Natives were to be conquered or controlled. This mindset was expressed in the Manifest Destiny advocated by our leaders throughout this period, and continued with the expansion of the nation to the west coast and the encroachment on the Mexican state.

Slavery, then, can be considered a tyrannical expression of our natural liberty, the boundless freedom of one group or person over others or another. The colonial expansion of the United States into the West shared this feature. Warfare upon the Native Americans and Mexicans further exemplified this unbridled liberty, untempered by morality or a sense of equality. There was little or no governance during the territorial expansion west of the Mississippi. It was truly the unlawful Wild West.

The slavery practiced in the southern territories west of the Appalachians, especially in Alabama, Mississippi, Louisiana, and Tennessee, was particularly harsh (13). Baptist's chronicle of the brutality of this period is poignant, including the forced marches into the southwest, whipping, torture, starvation, sexual exploitation, and forced labor practices (13). Although the slavery practiced in the new world might have been the most brutal, it should be clear from these analyses that slavery has been a feature of humanity throughout its existence. Further, the potential for a return of slavery is reinforced by the experience of the slave labor camps practiced during the Second World War, and the continued practice of slavery during Islamic Jihads in Africa and the Middle East and current sex-trafficking.

The Abolition of Slavery

Juxtaposed against the severity of the southern American slavery was a gradual mellowing of the attitudes of the European and northern United States toward black African slavery. Initially the transatlantic slave trade was incrementally eliminated, followed by international enforcement. Later, each of the colonial powers made slavery unlawful in their homelands. Finally, slavery was made unlawful in the African colonies themselves (14).

Presumably, the majority of Europeans, who reasoned that the institution of slavery was immoral, instigated these measures. Although slavery promoted the economic interests of their nations, it was considered unacceptable. As most political decisions are compromises between excess liberty and our ethical desire for some equality, slavery was gradually eliminated.

The moral sense in the United States also incrementally shifted against slavery, initially in the northern states, exemplified by the abolitionist movement. Most of the compromises initiated through this process were between the North's desire to restrict the expansion of slavery and the South's for further expansion. The Kansas-Nebraska Compromise implied that Nebraska would eventually be a free state and Kansas a slave state.

However, the Supreme Court's Dred Scott decision reinforced the concept that slaves were property, even when in "free" states. The political compromises and the courts during the 1850s altered major facets of the Missouri Compromise of 1820, which had previously restricted slavery's expansion. These changes suggested that slavery could potentially be expanded to all new territories, and that slaves of the southern slave states would remain slaves even when in the free states (15).

The distinctions among the four political parties with Abraham Lincoln's successful campaign for the presidency in 1860 were on slavery's expansion, not its elimination (15). During the war, it became clearer that slavery's abolition was a paramount reason for the war's continuance. The eventual emancipation by executive order ensued as a measure to induce the South's surrender.

Slavery, Liberty, and Equality

In some respects, the interplay between liberty and equality is evident in the world views of Andrew Jackson and Thomas Jefferson, respectively. Jackson and his followers favored maximizing freedom for white men at the expense of black Africans by encouraging slavery's expansion into the new territories. In addition, their advocacy of eliminating Native Americans from these territories by war and displacement was instrumental in this eventuality. Finally, Jackson's military leadership in the War of 1812 was critical to the success of the new Republic in maintaining control of New Orleans and the Mississippi River.

Thomas Jefferson, his followers, and, eventually, the abolitionists were restricted by the political realities described above. The economic expansion's dependence upon slavery, the survival of the Union, and the white Europeans' perception that black Africans were subhuman fostered the retention and expansion of slavery, until it was eliminated following the War Between the States. Jefferson and his followers were probably troubled by their failure to promote slavery's extinction and their allowing slavery's expansion through compromises, in spite of its immorality.

These politically immoral acts can be related to the natural course of individuals faced with moral challenges. Often, humans act immorally in spite of knowing better. Clearly Jefferson should have had qualms and feelings of guilt with his retention of his slaves and his behavior toward his black African mistress.

Yet, within the slavery culture of the South there were gradations of behavior between the dominant whites and the slaves as seen in the popular novels *Gone with the Wind* and *Uncle Tom's Cabin*. Some slaves were depicted within the family and community much more humanely in Margaret Mitchell's novel than displayed in Baptist's well-documented exposition (13, 16). Mitchell's novel was written well after the Civil War and supported the old South of Georgia. Although she can be viewed as an apologist for the South, her position cannot be ignored completely.

Written prior to the Civil War, Stowe's important novel described in detail some of the atrocities committed against slaves by their masters, but she also examined the lives of white men who behaved honorably when faced with the moral dilemma between supporting the structure of the community and its biases, politics, and economic realities; and the immorality of slavery (17).

Similarly, Tolstoy's Pierre Bezukhov, in *War and Peace*, exemplified this moral behavior by including some of his serfs in important functions, and, eventually, freeing his serfs. Although Russian serfs did not suffer the degree of ignominy experienced by the U.S. southern slaves, they shared many similarities (18).

Slavery's Aftermath

Following the Civil War, the slaves were freed constitutionally, reaffirming Lincoln's executive order, the Emancipation Proclamation. However, problems persisted and were inappropriately addressed. For the most part, the emancipated slaves were an uneducated underclass, with minimal skills. A system of indentured servitude was established, providing a method for African-Americans to eke out a living. Although legally enfranchised, most were restricted from voting by Jim Crow state laws. Separation of blacks from whites reinforced inequality in education, housing, and all the niceties of civil life.

The economic system of the South was also disrupted following the war. The cotton industry was not rejuvenated to the extent that it enjoyed under slavery. African-Americans working for a wage did not have the incentive to produce to the same extent that enforced slavery had, with its physical punishment and torture (19). Other industries were not available to replace those requiring slavery. Mississippi and Alabama remain among the poorest states of the union 160 years following the Civil War.

It took 100 years for the southern states to be forced to alter their Jim Crow laws and advance equality for African-Americans. The following sixty years have continued the process for both the North and the South.

It is instructive to look at the dissolution of slavery in other nations. The black African slave uprising in French Saint Domingue (later Haiti) in 1791 resulted in slavery's elimination. The new nation repulsed a large invasive force from the Napoleonic Empire in 1802 and has remained free of slavery. However, it has continued to be exploited by tyrannical regimes, led by black men rather than white. It remains one of the poorest nations on the planet (20).

Slavery's elimination in the remainder of the Americas was gradual and less convulsive than that of the United States. It was outlawed in the newly independent nations of Latin America in the 1820s. Mexico abolished slavery in 1824 and Brazil in 1831. Cuba eventually eliminated slavery in 1867. Similar to Haiti, most of the French-, Spanish-, and Portuguese-speaking nations of the Caribbean and Central and South American nations have remained poor compared to Europe, the United States, and Canada.

Although slavery might appear attractive to tyrannical autocracies, it is the best example of an extractive economy (21). These are economies that use their resources, including human capital, for the benefit of a small, elite group. Australia, Europe, Canada, and the northern United States have benefited from inclusive economies, those that provide opportunities for all of its members; capitalism flourishes when everyone potentially has a "stake in the game." These states have succeeded economically when compared to Africa, Latin America, the Middle East, and some of the southern United States. Slavery's prolonged involvement and its aftermath have been major factors in the poor economic development in these failed states and areas (21).

CONCLUSION

Slavery is a manifestation of our natural liberty superseding the promotion of equality. In this scenario, human liberty of some expands tyrannically over others in a desire to support their selves and their kin and clan, resulting in slavery. Biases, prejudices, and racism reinforce this process. Worldwide, the past three centuries have shown a gradual expansion of equality, reflecting our moral nature, politically restricting the freedom of some to advance equal treatment for all. As a result, slavery has been nearly eliminated. Both freedom and a desire for some equality are components of our nature. The balancing of these two aspects of our being play out politically.

No country, district, race or organized religion can excuse itself from involvement with slavery, as exemplified by the northern states' and Great Britain's engagement in the southern states' cotton-slavery industry; and the current use of slavery as a weapon in disputes among some black Africans. Slavery has been a blight on all of us, and on our human nature.

One might also conclude that the lovely words of Jefferson were expressed as a hope for the future. Allowing slavery's expansion during the first half century of our nation's history might be perceived as a necessary compromise to preserve the burgeoning Republic's unity, its sovereignty, and its economic development. Although United States' slavery was, perhaps, the most abhorrent example of slavery's iniquity, followed by a century of repression of those emancipated, slavery must be seen as a worldwide phenomenon, present throughout history to this day, an expression of unadulterated tyranny, an immoral exaggeration of our natural free will.

The history of the United States is marred by its past with slavery and its aftermath. However, the amelioration of these wrongs over the past half-century should be acknowledged. These accomplishments include the Emancipation Proclamation, the constitutional elimination of slavery, the expansion of liberty to African-Americans and women; the abolition of Jim Crow laws; Martin Luther King Day; and the election of an African-American President by a white majority. Guilt and shame over our past is appropriate. But just as appropriate, consistent with our country's background, is redemption.

Essay 4. War (1)

Except for ants and a few others, animals do not wage war within their species. Humans are exceptions to this rule, as war is clearly a human phenomenon. This can be related to features of our nature. To understand war it is instructive to investigate the geological and anthropological record of our species.

The age of mammals began in the Cenozoic Era, 65 millennia ago, following the catastrophic extinction of the dinosaurs. Our ancient, hominid ancestors are seen first in fossils dated 6.5 million years ago. The current ice age has been ongoing for the past 3 million years subsuming the Pleistocene Epoch. Our ice age has been characterized by long-lasting glaciations interrupted every 200,000 years or so by shorter, interglaciation warm periods, lasting 20,000-30,000 years (22).

The fossil record of Homo sapiens begins in Africa, Asia, and the Middle East, and dates from approximately 100,000 years BCE. The prior fossil record is scanty, although some have provided limited evidence of H. sapiens as early as 200,000 (23) and 300,000 years ago (24). Part of this difficulty is definitional, dependent upon how H. sapiens differs from other hominid species. The earliest European and American fossils are found much later. These fossil records support the contention that Hominids and Homo species began in Africa, thence to the Middle East, Australasia, and the Far East via land bridges from the last glaciation period. Entry into Europe and the Americas was limited due to the cold. Other hominids, including H. neanderthalensis and H. heidelbergensis, appear in European and American fossils earlier than H. sapiens' fossils.

The Holocene Epoch begins with the last closure of the land bridges and the current interglacial warm period, about 12,000 years ago. Presumably Homo sapiens were able to survive the northern cold during the onset of the interglacial, but before the Asia-Alaska land bridges closed. The earliest American H. sapiens' fossils are from this time.

At least 90% of H. sapiens' existence has been as hunter-gatherers during the last glaciation. The current interglacial warming period has been extant for only 12,000 years or so (22). It is important to note that there was coexistence of H. sapiens with other Homo species for the many thousands of years prior to the latters' extinctions. H. sapiens' survival success included dominance over all other forms of life, their spread across Earth, and the elimination of other hominids. This outstanding effort was due to H. sapiens' superior intellect and capacities to overcome the adversities of other species and the environment. This control of the environment, including the elimination of other hominids, was structured upon our aggressive tendencies and warfare against other species.

Some of the aggressive characteristics of our nature can be viewed as necessary for the fulfillment of our basic and biologic needs in an environment with limited resources. This was more apparent during humanity's earlier history during which much of our efforts had to be spent on survival. Most of the human characteristics have persisted. Virtues such as pride, competitiveness, property rights, honor, fidelity to kin and clan, and physical strength are manifestations of this component of our nature.

The downsides of this freedom are the restrictions of others' liberties. Our moral sense realizes that some liberties are immorally expressed (killing, stealing others' property, bullying, restricting others' speech or religious practices, etc.). Our individual behavior is often modulated from the extremes of liberty and bringing about fairness or justice. We modify the virtues of strength, courage, and honor with prudence, temperance, faith, charity, and stoicism. We can favor liberty and freedom yet foster some expansion of equality, thereby avoiding tyrannical expressions of unrestrained liberty on the one hand and the tyranny of the majority on the other.

A paradigmatic example for individual behavior might be the bully who is accosting one's sister. Clearly one should be courageous and face the bully, regardless of the potential physical harm to himself. However, the level of violence resulting from the action may be modified if circumstances allow. For example, the bully may cower in the face of opposition, allowing for a tempering of one's response. The courageous expression does not necessarily have to lead to bodily harm. One's courage can be modified by prudence and humility as it communicates strength.

These principles have been applied to the political arena, as we are social beings, manifested by our interactions with others, especially through the uniquely human facility of language. Legal institutions have been instituted which modify our individual freedoms. This is appropriate restriction of liberty, augmenting the moral expression of equality and diminishing the abuse of others' freedoms.

Turning to broader conflicts, we see that war has always been with us, related to limited natural resources and our aggressive nature. Looked at from the standpoint of clans and families struggling for subsistence while hunter-gatherers in forests and plains, one can realize that the cooperation among these smaller groups facilitated the groups' basic and broader needs. The preferential treatment of other members of the group fostered loyalty and feelings of duty. The encroachment of alien families and tribes and the eventuality of limited resources inevitably led to conflicts.

Whereas wars might have promoted some salutary effects including the virtues outlined above and by settling disputes, modern warfare has become extremely costly in terms of blood and treasure. Can anything justify the loss of the 40 million humans in World War II? Yet a world controlled by the grisly tyrants from Japan, Italy, Russia, and Germany would probably have been worse. Finally, the emergence of nuclear warfare makes future all-out warfare incomprehensible and suicidal. The asymmetrical nature of the more recent conflicts between larger nations and smaller entities raises additional difficulties. Clearly, it is preferable to resolve conflicts short of all-out war.

Evil has always existed, and benevolent societies should realize that defensive strength should be available. Although some religious traditions oppose violence at all costs, historical precedents have established that pacifism in every circumstance is not feasible. Further, religious traditions have promulgated some warfare, such as the many wars in the Old Testament, Christian Crusades, and Islamic jihads.

CONCLUSION

War, then, is a reflection of our natural freedom and our need to protect ourselves, clans, and nations from others who threaten to restrict our liberty. The evolutionary developments during the unpleasant environment of the last glaciation favored the success of our species, including our aggressive tendencies and warfare.

Similar to the courage used in confronting the bully in the individual example, societies should be able to deploy communal strength against opposing societies if all other measures fail. Sometimes the enunciation of strength is sufficient to dissuade others from aggressive behavior. Attempting to defuse conflicts through international bodies and having multinational involvement in conflict resolution should occur before force is instituted. Stronger nations should be tolerant of the weaker. Further proliferation of nuclear weaponry should be enjoined. Efforts to diminish the supply of weaponry to other nations should be advanced. Finally, if armed conflict ensues, limited and restricted ends should be pursued, and strategies for exiting the conflict should be delineated.

The track record for humanity's avoidance of war has not been good, but the stakes are currently much higher than in previous centuries. Similar to one's individual behavior when confronting evil in another individual, a nation or society can temper its response, without communicating cowardice or expressing irresoluteness. As bodily harm can be avoided in individual circumstances, war can be circumvented by judicious modification of each society's responses.

Essay 5. Shopping, Human Nature, and Male-Female Dynamic

When my wife of 50 years and I go shopping our experiences are at cross-purposes. This essay explores natural differences between the genders related to this experience.

As a boy, I occasionally went shopping with my mother. Before five minutes had elapsed I felt exhausted, my legs started to itch, and I began my search for a comfortable chair. Nowadays many department stores accommodate us grumbling men with waiting areas. I enjoy making friends and male camaraderie from this experience, but regret the absence of a barmaid. The best solution for this shopping disjunction is found in the streets of Old San Juan, Puerto Rico, where signs direct the wayward male to a neighborhood pub while the ladies go shopping.

As a rule, women love to shop; men generally view shopping with their ladies cruel and unusual punishment. Similar to shopping, driving instructions also distinguish the genders. Bud sends me a note to take route 43 north, turn left on Claremont Street, then go west two miles to Simonton. Turn right (north) and go about one mile. We are at 2250 on the right. Diane's instructions relate that Macy's is on the left before you turn left on Claremont. A Hobby Lobby store is on the right just before you turn on Simonton. After you go about a mile, we are at 2250, just after you pass a blue, Colonial home. For women, driving a car is another aspect of window shopping.

It is fruitful to study our species' early development to investigate natural versus cultural influences on these differences. According to fossil records, Homo sapiens have been present for at least 100,000 years, depending upon definitions. Some have suggested H. sapiens' presence as early as 300,000 years ago (23, 24). Earlier hominid species have been present for 6-7 million years, also dependent upon definitions, separating them from apes, bonobos, and chimpanzees.

Most of H. sapiens' existence has been during the last glaciation, which ended about 12,000 years ago, with the onset of the last interglacial warming period, which is ongoing, and the closure of the land bridges. Prior to the agricultural revolution and the establishment of towns and cities we were hunter-gatherers of the flora and fauna, struggling for survival (23).

Resources were limited during the hunter-gatherer period. Division of labor was an efficient system, allowing for sufficient food for individuals, families and clans. The larger, stronger male was better equipped for hunting. The female naturally turned to activities close to home, as she might be pregnant half of her child-bearing years. She also was charged with nurturing and suckling her young. Unlike robins, humans do not leave the nest before a decade has elapsed, due to slow maturation. As she was close to home, it was advantageous for her to gather edible plants and insects to eat or use for medicinal purposes. Her recognition of differences among leaves, stems, mushrooms, roots, and mosses refined her skills in these endeavors, including her social skills with other women.

The male, on the other hand, developed hunting abilities and teamwork to overcome the larger and faster fauna. He also was imbued with the virtues of honor and patriarchal sentiments, expressing commitment to protect and defend his family. The father taught his sons hunting and moral principles on how the boy becomes a man. The mother developed judgments regarding the value of things, enhancing her bartering ability, and she taught these skills to her children.

Augmented hunting expertise among the men, and gathering acumen among the women improved survival for the family and clan. Any beneficial genetic predisposition would more likely be preserved in those surviving. Genetic preferences for these abilities were reinforced with each generation. Those more suitably adapted to the hostile environment lived long enough to reproduce children with these genetic traits.

The shopping skills of women reflect these gathering tendencies. Gentlemen, you should embrace your spouse's shopping skills, whether in a store or in driving, as she is cataloguing information for you and your family. The engaging pricing process simply refines her skills in modern bartering activities, increasing the value of purchases.

The likelihood of significant genetic determinants in these and other skills does not diminish cultural impacts. One can appreciate the marked cultural changes in Western societies in male-female dynamics over the past two centuries. No longer are women restricted from activities and freedoms previously reserved for men: enfranchisement, expanded employment opportunities, access to educational experiences, legal protection from predatory males, sexual liberty, among others. All of these gains should be applauded as they enhance liberty, which is one of the paramount features of our nature. However, the exercise of these liberties is not formulaic, as each individual is unique. All ought to navigate life in accord with their own dispositions, moral nature, responsibilities, and physical limitations. The lesson from this essay underscores the importance of natural, genetically determined, aspects of male-female interactions, exemplified by a somewhat whimsical discussion of shopping. We should not forget that we are biologic beings.

The natural, hunter aspect of males is evident as he gains pride and self-respect in his work. Virtues such as courage, humility, and honor are on display in these activities. Patriarchal urges to protect his wife and family is an extension of this perception. A large component is his functioning as a role model for his sons and daughters. The converse is evident when he loses his job and wallows in his despondency.

The gatherer aspect of women is present as she makes her home beautiful, and gives birth to and nurtures her children, gaining fulfillment. Shopping is one manifestation of this process.

The recent cultural changes in our society have proceeded without appropriate considerations of our biologic nature. Some of these between the genders might be detrimental individually and politically, exemplified by the disruption of some families, with no male role-models. Ideally, men should teach their sons and daughters what it is to be a man. Some cultural changes between the sexes have proceeded much more rapidly than biologic accommodation.

Biologic, or genetic, modifications do occur in species, especially if they produce survival advantages to their offspring, but the evolution proceeds slowly. There are examples of human characteristics that have diminished survival value but persist. Homosexuality is an obvious example, as it limits procreation. However, it remains in all human societies. It could be argued that this sexual orientation is solely cultural, although many homosexuals feel that their sexual preference preceded much cultural input.

Clear-cut genetic disorders, such as Down's syndrome, bring home the point better. The incidence of Down's syndrome does not appear to be decreasing in spite of its genetic disadvantage. Of course, genetic determinism can be very complex, and there may be genetically linked alleles, some salutary and some not. Nevertheless, these two examples show the slow process of genetic change in humans.

It should not surprise us, then, that the increased freedom for women has been accompanied by tensions between the sexes. Two examples clarify this issue. Recently, Dr. Koven wrote a nice editorial exploring the dynamic between the cultural changes and our biology in the relative complement of male and female physicians (25). She was a brave pioneer in medicine, before much of the cultural changes had ensued. She indicated that she often felt wounded when her patients did poorly. Unlike many of her male counterparts, she related empathically with her patients. She had some difficulties conforming to the "macho" style of the men in her chosen subspecialty, gastroenterology. I was warmed by her final realization that her individual qualities are those of an excellent physician.

Dr. Koven's reactions to the cultural changes that have occurred between the genders in medicine is understandable. She should realize that H. sapiens have been present for at least 100,000 years. The salutary, fundamental expansion of freedom for women has occurred during the past two centuries, just 0.002 of H. sapiens' existence. Based upon the hunter-gatherer, genetic predispositions outlined above, it is understandable that women usually relate more naturally and empathically to their patients; men in a more authoritarian manner. Each physician is unique and has to find his or her role in this spectrum. Self-examination is part of this process. Her personal traits are precisely what patients desire in their physicians. On the other hand, a competent physician needs to be authoritarian when required. Male and female physicians need to adopt both features.

Secondly, recently an Uber female executive commented that she was pleased that a second woman was elected to its board of directors. A male executive countered, tongue-in-cheek, that at least there will be more talking during the board meetings. He was then categorized as sexist and consequently apologized for the indiscretion.

Neither the sexist characterization nor the apology was appropriate. I think that most agree that women generally are more socially adept than men. If we accept the formulation that women were the "gatherers" during most of our species existence, it follows that socializing is a trait of the "gatherers." She had the opportunity to join in the humor with the "perfect squelch," that finally they will get something done through compromise rather than suffer through male hubris, posturing, and pride.

Another approach is to recognize and celebrate the differences between the sexes. Successful marital couples learn this early in their lives together. Men like to congregate over sporting activities, which reflect their hunter, competitive nature. Women commonly enjoy social interactions like book clubs, sewing and knitting, quilting groups, and simply "jawing" with other women. None of these generalizations are absolute but we all can appreciate the differences. It is advisable for couples to accommodate to these realities.

A more serious matter is in sexual relations between the sexes. With the emancipation of women during the past century, the rules of engagement between the sexes have become muddied. During the Victorian age a single woman might have been considered "loose" if she went for a walk with a man unaccompanied by a chaperone. Currently, some find any sexual behavior, such as "hooking up," acceptable behavior. How do parents advise their children? Are sexual activities to be taken no more seriously than other physiologic functions, such as having a bowel movement? With the loosening of sexual mores, how is rape or sexual harassment defined?

In this controversy it is wise to realize that we are biologic creatures with natural tendencies. Men generally want to be protective of their women and families. They want to be considered special by their partner. A woman wants to feel protected by her spouse or boyfriend, and that he is faithful to her and her family. Matters of sexuality are profound and ought to be taken very seriously. Sexual intercourse without intimacy is not intimate.

CONCLUSION

This discussion of male-female differences was introduced by showing that one's experience of shopping is generally different between the sexes. This was related to our genetic nature, mostly developed when our species was comprised of hunter-gatherers. The discussion continued by exploring the contrast between the rapid cultural changes between the sexes and our plodding biology.

Essay 6. Free Will and the Physical World: The Mind-Body Quandary

The physical world is the world of our senses, described in causal, everyday language and made intelligible by science. As infants, we apprehend that we can see, touch, hold, smell, hear and taste the physical world, and that our senses complement one another. The tactile shape confirms the visual appearance of a thing. Tasting embellishes the pleasant odor of food. Sometimes one sense modifies our judgment of the physical world ascertained by another sense, as when touch confirms the straightness of a stick in water that is refractively bent as sensed by vision.

The process of experiencing the physical world includes both the sensations and the inferences made about the sensations, which clarify the world. We infer or induce concepts in explaining the world. Concepts of causality, time, space and gravity are not seen directly. Rather they are the fabric of experiences. Things that we sense are contained within space and time, but space and time are not directly felt. Gravity is always with us, but we do not touch it directly. Rather, we note the glass crashing to the floor, the strain on our bodies while getting up, the acorn falling from the oak tree. Causality is inferred, as we do not see causality as one billiard ball strikes another; rather, we see the first billiard ball striking the second, then the second moving from the first.

The common-sense descriptions of the world are provided by everyday language, consensually reinforced by other people. The words are signs, representing things, and are agreed upon by the use of the same language, a product of our social nature. Involving a third human or a dictionary can often resolve differences of opinions between two humans on things, as the meanings are established by consensus.

The scientific approach to the world uses different procedures in its quest to understand and explain physical processes. Precise measurements of phenomena and mathematical descriptions are components of the techniques involved. Sophisticated technologies are also involved. Often, statistical inferences are made. The usefulness of a theoretical description is measured by the extent to which it provides a deeper understanding of a phenomenon. Further, the theoretical descriptions often allow for predictions of future events. The language of science is couched in the inference that the physical world behaves in a causal manner, similar to the common-sense language.

The distinction between seeing red and the physical description of the accompanying physical, chemical, and neurological events is readily apparent. When we first understand redness, it is a color present on an object. Infants become accustomed to notions of redness by pointing at objects and by the consensual use of the description, red. Gradations of redness occur as red blends into orange. No one can claim that his perception of red is identical to another's, as no one can get inside another's mind to see what the other sees. However, there are enough similarities in what is called red to allow for a mutual understanding of redness, expressed in common-sense, everyday language. Colorblindness in some can be clarified by enlisting the involvement of those who are not colorblind.

On the other hand, if technology were sufficiently advanced, it might be theoretically possible to have an external imaging technique directed at one's brain that would be able to completely describe all of the physical, chemical, and neurological events taking place while someone sees red. However, the physical accounting of the process is distinctly different from the common-sense meaning of perceiving red.

When a human physical action is performed, both common-sense and scientific languages can elucidate it, but the two depictions are quite different. The scientific explanation – including neurological, neurochemical, and physical descriptions – is different from the common-sense account of the action. The first is potentially an external study of the physical processes involved; the second involves the internal self engaged in the action.

The distinction between one's self and the neurochemical apparatus that accompanies self-hood can be explicated by some homely examples, such as honking a horn. While driving down a street with your spouse, you honk your horn. Your spouse saw a squirrel scurrying across the street 50 feet away and commented that the honking was unnecessary as the squirrel would have been safely across the street before you would get to it. You reply that you were not honking at the squirrel; rather you were saying hello to your neighbor, Joe, who was raking leaves. Let's imagine that a set of scans are available that could have been directed at your brain and would completely describe all of the physical, neuronal, and chemical processes going on before and after your honking. No matter how thorough, the external scientific review would not get at the reason for the action.

Clearly, the descriptions of the event would be different. Included in the common-sense narration were many things not included in the scientific explanation (honking expressing warning and greeting, depending upon the reason; the disregard of the squirrel's importance; the reason itself). Only a statement in common-sense language explains the action, although the scientific elaboration can describe the hardware involved.

Let's assume that the physical process accompanying the action is different if the reason for the action is different. That would argue that there is a closer correspondence between the common-sense and the scientific descriptions, when obviously they are very different. No matter how close the correspondence, the two languages describe different things. Further, envisioning programming a physical process beforehand corresponding perfectly with the host of potential reasons is daunting. One can hypothesize a computer-like physicochemical processor in the brain in which language could be translated, but it is difficult to envision a program that would include a potential infinity of reasons for an action.

A simpler rendering of this mind/body conundrum is to accept the obvious duality. The mind or the self is not the same as the accompanied bodily expressions. However, each can interact with and cause a reaction in the other, sometimes simultaneously. Dreams are a reshuffling of our memories, which appear in a type of consciousness, or subconsciousness, that is not under conscious control. We cannot control our dreams. Memories can likewise spontaneously enter our wakeful, conscious minds. Conversely our conscious minds are free to bring up memories. Our selves can cause physical processes in our brains and neuromuscular systems when we do something. Our memories stored in our physical brains can cause conscious events in our minds.

The nexus between the mind and body, mostly the brain, is not clear, but it clearly exists. In the same sense that we do not see the causal nexus between two physical events, we induce or infer it.

Inherent in doing an action for a reason are the notions of freedom and responsibility. It is assumed that we could have done otherwise when we perform an action freely. Since we choose to do the action, we have responsibility for it. Some reflex activities are best described by external causation rather than by personal reasons for the events. For example, you pull your hand away when you put it on a hot stove. You are not expressing freedom, as the reaction was outside of your control. Likewise, you cannot be held responsible for the episode.

There are many intermediary circumstances of compulsions, biases, and prejudices that are genetically and culturally derived over which you have less freedom. Your freedom is more obviously expressed when you act in opposition to these biases. Similarly, freedom and responsibility are displayed more prominently when you are being forced to do something against your will and you refuse to do it.

How does this formulation deal with the social sciences of sociology, anthropology, psychology, and economics? Sociological and anthropological sciences study groups of humans in aggregate and compare their behavior to other groups. Often, statistical comparisons and inferences are made. There is a tacit implication that there is a loss of freedom in the group's behavior, and that explanations are best made causally. Also implied is a loss of responsibility for the group, as its behavior is caused by various factors, including genetics and acculturation. The group is compelled to behave in a certain way. Economic theories of behavior have similar assumptions.

Two important aspects of these behavioral sciences need to be inspected more closely. First, human groups are comprised of individual free agents. Although groups of individuals seem to act in a certain manner, there remains an unpredictable element due to freedom exercised by the group's individuals. This is seen prominently in economic theory with the unpredictability of "bubbles," the uncertainty of the direction of the stock market, etc.

Human free will and group behavior can be compared metaphorically to the individual electron within its atomic electron cloud. Although the electron cloud can be described by statistical, quantum mechanics, the precise location of the individual electron cannot be placed. Group behavior is analogous to the electron cloud, while individual free will is like the individual electron's location.

The electron has a type of freedom, although of a different sort than human free will. The electron's freedom is a type of unpredictability, which is quite different from human free action. Absolute unpredictability in human actions is devoid of responsibility. One exercises his free will when he makes thoughtful decisions for which he takes responsibility.

The second issue involves language. When a group or a culture has a specific language and social structure explained in that language, it is difficult for an outside observer, with a different native language and cultural heritage, to differentiate individual actions from actions as a group, unless the outside observer embroils himself in the culture and language. This becomes more difficult when various cultures are compared, as each culture has unique characteristics. An apparent bias observed by an outside observer would not necessarily be considered a bias within the studied culture. Reasons for a group's or culture's actions are best understood within that culture.

CONCLUSION

There are two quite different entities in our world: the scientifically observable, physical one; and the world of the mind, consciousness, and free will. The former can be described by causal language, or, in the atomic strata, by probability. Free will, then, is able to make an imprint in the world that is not caused fundamentally by the physical world, but is instigated by free action, described by reasons for the action, not by causes of the action. In a sense, the causal universe folds around the instigation and goes about its causal business, as if nothing happened.

SECTION II. EPISTEMOLOGY; HOW DO WE THINK? WHAT IS TRUE OR REASONABLE?

This section continues the discussion of our nature and of our reasoning capacity. In many respects this section is an extension of the last. The two essays explore many of the concepts in Essay 1, Human Nature. The first on metaphysics draws on the distinctions between our usual reasoning and metaphysics, and in what circumstances they are conjoined. Essay 8 uses the ancient tale of the tortoise and the hare to characterize types of reasoning, how they sometimes come into conflict, and how common-sense thinking clarifies the controversies.

Essay 7. Does Metaphysics Belong in Philosophical Discourse?

Introduction

This essay examines the relationships between metaphysics and philosophy. First, paradigmatic examples of metaphysics are presented. These are counterpoised against our common-sense, deductive, inductive, and linguistic reasoning capacities. Then, some intermediate positions between metaphysics and conventional reasoning are adduced. In the light of this discussion, dreams and inspiration are explored. Finally, conclusions are drawn on the place of metaphysical considerations in philosophy.

Metaphysics, definition

William James pronounced that the most consequential philosophical issue is between the "one" and the "many": whether the world is unitary or pluralistic (26). Whereas his pronouncement and confession that he was a pluralist were done as a rejection of the Hegelian philosophy, one might also regard his statement as metaphysical, outside of the conventional purview of philosophical discourse.

A reasonable definition of metaphysics is a field of purported knowledge, generally expounded in terms of mystical or supernatural beliefs, outside of our common-sense language, our scientific language, and our usual understanding of our selves within the world. In short, it is an exploration of areas foreign to our usual common-sense or scientific discourse. Two metaphysical examples can serve as introductions to the topic.

The first is Abraham's decision to sacrifice his son, Isaac, as instructed by God. No one observed the interaction between God and Abraham. In spite of this decision, he continued to believe that Isaac would somehow live. Soren Kierkegaard explored this paradox in his book, *Fear and Trembling*, explaining it in terms of a "leap of faith."

The second example is someone claiming to see the Virgin Mary at Lourdes, with no witnesses to the event. This claim transcends our everyday experience and was not verified by others.

Can truth be ascribed to either of these claims? The epistemological question is meaningless unless we have the ability to seek truth, which, in turn, demands an understanding of our nature. If we do not have the capability to look for truth with our natural resources, there is no sense in engaging in the exercise.

Natural Modes of Reasoning

The ability to think and to reason is, then, a requirement for epistemic investigation. However, we are unable to prove reason by using our reason. We must accept reasoning as a component of our nature. Introspection and interactions with others reinforce our belief in our thinking ability.

There are three ways in which we reason. First is our deductive ability, characterized by logic and the syllogism, exemplified by our mathematical and much of our scientific thinking.

The second is by induction by which we make inferences, which make sense of the world. The inferences are applied to our experiences, providing generalizations. One inference, early in our lives, is our appreciation that there are things in the world, which are interpretations of the sensual data that we receive. The different experiences complement one another in this process. The red ball looks different from a distance than close. Its three dimensions are confirmed by touch. It is inferred to be a red ball, based on the many experiences of redness and of round balls. This process is assisted by interactions with other people.

Both our common-sense and scientific inductions are described in consensually agreed upon languages. A third person or a dictionary can clarify differences of opinions about things and inferences. This linguistic clarification of words and meanings is the third manner in which we think or use our reason.

Metaphysical Statements

Metaphysical statements are of a different sort. They are not deductive, scientific, nor common-sense utterances that can be verified by others and can be discussed in these agreed-upon languages. In addition, they are not inferences about us and the world that can be independently verified by others. Finally, they are not simple clarifications of the meaning of the statements, performed within a mutual language. Rather, metaphysical pronouncements are individualistic statements about supernatural entities or ideas, often employing languages different from the above.

By itself, the individualistic aspect does not make it metaphysical. When things are observed, felt, reasoned, or asserted, they are individual experiences. No one can tell what is in another's mind. Each human's thoughts are unique. However, the conveyance of thoughts requires commonality of expression. The red ball is understood as redness and balls are used in our usual language. No one knows if each observer sees the red ball identically, but each agrees that the object in question is a red ball. Scientific discussions proceed similarly, with agreement among the discussants. Clarifications can occur within the language used if there is disagreement with an observation or its interpretation. Even though each of our thoughts is individualistic, there is a commonality among those sharing the experience. The individualism expressed by metaphysical statements is different.

The two metaphysical examples given contain the individualistic element of all thoughts, but they do not share the experience that is reasonably expressed in common sense or scientific language. Abraham's contention is unreasonable, as it defies deductive logic. One cannot be both alive and dead, simultaneously. Likewise, the vision of the Virgin Mary, unseen by anyone else, is extraordinary and incomprehensible for most.

Intermediary Situations

There are some intermediary situations, such as group prayer, wherein agreed-upon constructions are displayed in religious organizations. Common understandings are shared within the groups. Religious beliefs in a deity or deities are expressed in the same language. In many respects, the language and interactions are similar to common-sense language and activities, but the tenets or belief systems are different. Common-sense and scientific languages are based on objective experience of the world, using rules based on deductive and inductive reasoning. Most religious belief systems are grounded on ideas that are supernatural, hence metaphysical, concepts. Deities, fate, magic, and an afterlife are belief systems that meet this criterion. Although deductive reasoning and inductive inferences are used similarly to those made about the natural world, the subject of the discourse is different.

Some supernatural belief systems are related to the world and are alternative explanations of phenomena, using mystical elements. Some have been abandoned as scientific knowledge has progressed. Scientific explanations for lightning and thunder have superseded explanations involving angry deities. There are some that are founded on scientific study and are not so easily discarded. For example, the exquisite anatomy of the eye and the complex physiology of vision might suggest teleology, implying design and a Designer. These teleological ideas might be circumvented as our understanding of biology unfolds, and concepts of evolution, natural selection, and mutations are advanced.

Some religious, magical, or supernatural beliefs have been a feature of all cultures and are best considered components of our nature. It is natural for us to raise questions that are not explained by the common-sense language of the world. What preceded the big bang, in cosmological theory? Why are we here? Why is there something rather than nothing? These are clearly metaphysical questions.

Since inferences about the natural world are not directly experienced, there is an element of the supernatural in our everyday explanations. Making sense of the world with inferences and induction is a major component of our reasoning capacity. For example, our claim that something causes something else is not directly experienced, but the induction makes sense of the constant connection observed. Causality is the basic principle employed in scientific elucidation.

Likewise, concepts of space, time, and gravity are not directly identified. They are the fabric of the objective world and are components of its description. The difference between these constructs and the metaphysical is that the latter are not about the physical world. Rather, the beliefs and explanations are about supernatural entities.

There are two components of the world that seem to bridge the natural and supernatural. The first is the characterization of the subatomic world by quantum mechanics. According to particle physics theory, the position of an electron within an atomic electron cloud can only be indicated by a statistical probability. Its location is "superimposed" in multiple locations simultaneously until it is "measured." Further there is an uncertainty principle regarding elemental particles that their momenta (or velocities) cannot be identified simultaneously with their locations. Both of these theoretical positions are contrary to both standard, scientific thinking and common-sense discourse. The usual causal explanations do not seem to hold up in the subatomic sphere. However, causality remains reliable in the aggregate, the commonly observed world.

The second is free will. In an entirely deterministic universe, human activity could conceivably be described entirely in causal terms. In principle, if free will were not present, all human action could be predicted infallibly. However, an examination of our nature reveals that we are free to choose among actions. We discuss and explain these actions in terms of reasons for the actions, not causes. A common-sense language is used instead of a scientific one.

There are physical processes accompanying these free actions. If I want to explain my walking to the local voting booth, filling out a ballot and placing the ballot in the ballot box, I do it in common-sense language, using these terms. The physicochemical and physiological processes involved with walking, writing, and placing the ballot can be described, potentially, in scientific, causal language. The reasons for the action, described in common-sense language, are different from the elaborate, scientific, causal description. The latter is always incomplete in characterizing reasons for free action.

Further, the junction between the will to do something and the physical doing is not observed. The nexus is inferred or induced in order to make the action understandable. Our free action causes the physical occurrence, but the physical world does not cause us to act when we act freely.

We are not acting freely when we are forced to do something reflexly, such as drawing our hand away from a hot stove. We are cognizant of the event, but we neither cause nor take responsibility for it. The amount of freedom is related inversely to the degree of compulsion. In a reflex, we are compelled to do something and it is not a component of our free will. Similarly, a schizophrenic responding to a hallucinated command is not acting freely. On the other hand, refusal to do something that a tyrant is demanding demonstrates the highest degree of freedom. Regardless of the type of human activity, changes are caused in the physical world. When freely done, one's self causes the physical changes.

Similarly, the world that we experience in our daily lives is not affected by the unpredictability of occurrences in the subatomic world. The element of chance or probability with elemental particles is averaged or smoothed out in the conventional world of daily experience. The freedom displayed by subatomic particles is distinctly different from human free will. If our actions were entirely unpredictable, occurring by chance alone, we would not be responsible for them, nor would they be free.

Returning to our essay, we need to relate human free will and random occurrences of subatomic particles to our preliminary definition of metaphysics. Human free will is observed and experienced in our everyday life, and it is described in terms of giving reasons for actions. Freedom is one of the foremost characteristics of our nature. Its acceptance is clearly not metaphysical, as it is grounded in our daily activities, does not invoke a supernatural entity that others do not observe, and is expressed in our consensual language

The behavior of particles in the subatomic world, as described by quantum mechanics, is counterintuitive, as the theory implies that an object's location cannot be identified with certainty, but only probabilistically. However, the particle's behavior is described in scientific language and the theoretical descriptions are testable by accepted, scientific investigations. Although the subatomic world is strange when compared to our usual experiences, it is not metaphysical.

There are gradations among various methods of discourse and experiences involving metaphysics. Characteristics of metaphysics involve language other than our common-sense, linguistic analysis, and scientific varieties. Individualistic pronouncements and beliefs are used that are not shared by others. Supernatural descriptions are outside of the natural world of human experience.

Perhaps the most difficult challenge for a philosopher looking at metaphysical questions is distinguishing a metaphysical experience from an hallucination or delusion. If a psychiatrist, a modern-day philosopher, or scientist were to interview Bernadette following her experiences at Lourdes or Abraham's narrating his beliefs, both would probably be considered delusional and schizophrenic. These would be reasonable judgments, as the pronouncements and beliefs uttered are truly metaphysical. However, these judgments would be at variance with many of the belief systems of the Judeo-Christian traditions. Although unreasonable, Abraham's and Bernadette's stories ring true to some.

Eternal Sleep

Dreams and inspiration have some metaphysical overlap with conventional reasoning. They have elements in their intersections with our common-sense appreciation of the world. Hamlet's soliloquy on death and dreaming brings up several issues. When we have a dreamless sleep, we lose awareness, consciousness, and self-consciousness – the closest experience we have to eternal death, in the ultimate sense, assuming death is the end of all consciousness. Dreamless sleep is timeless, as there is no sense (consciousness) of time during that interval. Each episode might have been a minute or a century, had we no external corroboration of time's passage during the interval of sleep. There is a refreshing aspect to a "good night's sleep," which is reflected in Hamlet's suggestion that a dreamless sleep would be preferred to the travails of our conscious existence.

Whereas Hamlet felt that this dreamless sleep is welcomed, most shudder at the prospect of eternal nothingness, not only for the billions of years for our universe to collapse or expand relentlessly into vacant space, but for eternity, forever. Our world would likewise collapse, as each of us has his own, unique experience of the world.

Hamlet feared the frightful dreams that might accompany death, although he was using dreams metaphorically for a non-corporeal afterlife. However, most religious concepts of an afterlife are rendered as a type of existence similar to life on Earth. Imagining our selves divorced from our bodies is difficult. Our very nature is hinged upon our being in our bodies, with the external world, time, space, gravity, causality, and other people. Passively, we receive messages into our consciousness from our physical bodies and the universe, and we act upon their physical presence in the world. One is hard-put to find elements of our consciousness completely separate from the world.

Our memories are related to dreams and our conscious selves, although they are distinct. The memory stores that which we have experienced, done, thought, learned, and dreamt, and, in many respects, represents us, but it is not identical to ourselves, as it is not the active agent of our self-expression. Memories can enter our consciousness passively, as they do in our dreams, and, sometimes, in our wakeful consciousness. But our conscious selves can also bring up memories willfully. Conscious memories enter consciousness both volitionally and passively, whereas dreams only arrive unintentionally.

Memory is the storage capacity and the physical components of our conscious selves and our dreams. There is a reciprocal causation between the physical elements, our memories; and ourselves, our consciousness, our being. When we act in the world, we cause an activation of our memories. When we bring up memories volitionally, we cause our memories to be brought into consciousness. When memories spontaneously appear, they are apprehended in our consciousness. Dreams, on the other hand, have a one-way causation from our memories to our "unconscious consciousness." Similar to other passive perceptions, the dream state enters our consciousness. Unlike our conscious selves who have freedom to act in the world, a dream has no willful components, clearly different from the conscious states with their panoply of active and passive involvement.

In contradistinction to the Everly Brothers' contention that they could cause a dream of their loved one anytime (27), dreams enter our "unconscious consciousness," or subconscious, spontaneously, similar to sensory inputs into our consciousness. The dream state differs from our consciousness in the world, as we are active participants in the world, but solely passive recipients in dreams. We have no freedom over or responsibility for our dreams. Dreams are intermediate between our consciousness and the physical world.

Psychoanalytic disciplines, especially those of Sigmund Freud, have stressed the importance of dreams in analyzing psychopathology. Some of his conclusions regarding the unconscious or subconscious mind – including his depiction of the ego, superego, and id – suggest metaphysical formulations.

Hamlet might not fear dreams that are simply caused by the physical presence of memory, a reshuffling of imprints within our physical brains, and entering our dreams. However, he did fear the nightmares occurring during death, endless sleep, in a metaphysical sense, perhaps his version of hell.

Our universal beliefs in, or longing for, existence beyond our mortal lives, then, do not coincide with either a dreamlike state or our terrestrial state, both of which are dependent upon the physical world of bodies, memories, and the external world. A disembodied consciousness is difficult to conceptualize. Yet our desire for immortality is overwhelming, perhaps the most fundamental characteristic of our being. Much of our literature, religious thought, poetry, music, and visual art derives from this aspect of our nature, and realizes our human dignity and humility.

Regardless of our lives' ends, each of us apprehends how special each of our conscious selves is, different in all respects to, but dependent upon, the physical universe.

Unlike Hamlet, who feared dreams interrupting his eternal sleep, most of us experience dread from eternal nothingness, to the extent that we cannot envision the world without our presence.

Inspiration

Similar to dreams, inspiration shares some aspects of metaphysics. The conceptualization of the benzene ring may have been captured by the organic chemist, August Kekulé, in his sleep or daydream. One carbon atom was envisioned engulfed by the sixth atom, like a snake eating its tail. In sleep, some have "dreamt-up" solutions to poetic, musical or artistic problems. Others have commented that their ideas appear in their sleep. One can consider these events inspired. Whereas they might be simple, random reshuffling of our memories, they suggest a loftier stature. Mozart's prolific output of musical loveliness, Da Vinci's depiction of the Mona Lisa smile and his other momentous works of art, and Newton's and Einstein's crafting of their theories on motion were expressions of inspiration, seemingly appearing uniquely in their minds. One might wonder how these novel developments came about.

Clearly, they were dependent upon previous experiences, incorporated in their memories, as they would have to have aural and visual input, which would allow expression through a common-sense or scientific language. Further, an understanding of previous scientific or artistic achievements would be required. In addition, the human intuitive capacity to put things together to create fresh interpretations of things is necessary, but inspiration seems to exceed the simple principles of inference.

On a more basic level, inspiration would also have to be dependent on aspects of our nature: our rationality, freedom, moral sense, luxuriant bed of emotions, and our cognizance of beauty. These features are, at least, under genetic control and are modified by education and training. The mix of these aspects of our nature differs considerably among us. For scientific inspiration, one would need to have a strong, rational, deductive, thinking capacity that would also be capable of inference outside of the mainstream.

On the other hand, artistic inspiration is more related to a heightened aesthetic sense. The religious and philosophical insight that C. S. Lewis expressed while observing the stark, bare, trees against the winter night-time sky stimulated some of his feelings toward the supernatural (28). The resounding grief expressed in the plaintive poem by Tennyson, "But, oh, for the touch of a vanished hand, Or the sound of a voice that is still," resonates much more fully in someone who might be inspired to write great poetry (29). Listening to the ineffable loveliness of a Mozart piano concerto, Franz Liszt may have experienced the foundation for his revolutionary, inspired music.

In addition to these aspects of our nature, it is also necessary for inspiration to develop upon the background of our memories. Memories comprise the storage mechanism of all that we have experienced, emoted, thought and remembered.

The process of inspiration, then, is complex, dependent upon our nature as its soil, and both conscious effort and unconscious activity. The stratum for inspiration is the organic core of our memories. We voluntarily bring up into consciousness aspects of our memory, including vocabulary, events, experiences, and emotions. Some things in our memory appear spontaneously, contributing to the inspirational effort. Novel insights or artistic expressions result. Some of these inspirational creations are initiated in our sleep in dreams, eventually transcribed in our conscious minds. Inference, induction, and generalizations are under both voluntary and involuntary control. We call those that are mostly involuntary, inspiration.

Although the reshuffling of aspects of our memory is a large component of the inspirational process, there are also components of our consciousness that are not translatable into obviously storable items within our organic memories. A poem can induce a feeling in our conscious mind that is more than the words themselves. It is easy to visualize a computer-like memory storage device that could serve language. But that memory would be less than the entire conscious feeling that the poem induces. True inspiration, then, comprises mental exercises in addition to the reshuffling of memory, consciously or unconsciously. Although memory provides the tools for inspirational insight, it does not explain the entire picture.

Is There a Place for Metaphysics in Philosophy?

Logical positivists and other modern thinkers have indicated that metaphysical propositions are meaningless, as they cannot be verified. However, absolute verification of our inferences, including reason itself, is not possible. Returning to William James' philosophical discussions on non-verifiable issues, his reaction to the Hegelian philosophy (of the "one" school), is filled with his philosophical insights, including scholarly praise of Bergson and Peirce (of the "many" school) (26).

Appropriately, philosophy contains some metaphysical elements, including inferences made that are partly within and partly without the natural world. It discusses belief systems that are clearly supernatural, and asserts that the metaphysical discussion is a legitimate component of our nature. Further, common-sense or scientific language is used in discussing some supernatural beliefs. Science can generate some metaphysical considerations, such as teleological descriptions suggesting design and a Designer.

Robert M. Craig, M.D.

The breathtaking beauty of a Puccini love duet, the pain from the loss of your innocent child, or the awesome grandeur in contemplating the majesty of our universe cannot be treated alone by common-sense, scientific, or analytic thinking. Finally, metaphysical questions: such as what is truth, why are we here, is there life after death, and what preceded the big bang, are raised by the thoughtful philosopher, navigating the understanding of the world and our nature. Although many of these questions are best treated with poetry, music, or the visual arts, which are languages of the heart rather than the brain, they also reside in the province of the philosopher.

Essay 8. The Tortoise and the Hare

There is an old tale, dating from the ancient Greeks, which has been duplicated in other fables, that I shall call "The Tortoise and the Hare." Although the usual story involves a lazy rabbit who oversleeps and allows the tortoise to win, there is another, more philosophical, rendition.

In this version the pompous hare indicates that, in spite of giving the tortoise a large lead, he still will beat the tortoise to the finish line easily. The tortoise explains that he cannot possibly be overtaken in this contest and explains, "You see, as you run to overtake me, you have to cover half of the distance first. Then you have to cover half of the remaining distance and so on, into an infinite regression. There will always be another half to overcome before the complete distance is covered."

The logic is unassailable but, of course, the hare overtakes the tortoise and wins the race. Why is our logical presentation in opposition to what we know by our common-sense and everyday experience? Knowing that a hare is faster than a tortoise, we also know that the hare will pass the tortoise in a race. Observing behaviors of tortoises and hares provides empirical support for our belief. What is wrong with our logic?

How Do We Think?

An examination of how we think is required. First, it is tautological that we use reason in this effort. Reasonableness is necessary, otherwise it is senseless to pursue what is reasonable or true. To reason is to examine the truthfulness of propositions.

We naturally have three modes of reasoning. The first is deductive, which entails logical analysis based upon accepted axioms. It uses its fundamental principles in mathematics, the sciences, and common sense.

The second is inductive whereby we infer principles or facts that make sense of the world. Some of our earliest inductions or inferences are directly experienced: the self and self-consciousness, the physical world, and our ability to act in the physical world. Other inferences are not directly experienced, but are the common-sense notions of gravity, time, space, and causality. Scientific thinking also uses induction in its theories to explain phenomena.

The third is through analysis of language and its meaning. Often misunderstandings or fallacies are clarified by the use of a dictionary or a third person to referee disagreements.

None of these methods of reason is infallible. Logic is dependent upon the axioms employed. Parallel lines cannot meet in plane geometry, yet they can in spherical geometry. Also, logical systems may contain truths outside of those directly obtained from their defined axioms and operations, so-called metamathematics, as displayed in Gödel's Proof (4).

Likewise, inferences are always tentative and can be modified when new empirical information becomes available. These inferences are not directly observed. Rather, they clarify the world. We do not directly experience time, causality, space, or gravity. Instead, they are the fabric of our experience.

Although there is a tentative aspect to each of these modes of reasoning, thinking reasonably is the unifying principle that allows us to adjudicate rightness vs. wrongness, or truth vs. falsehood. Reason is the starting point. It supersedes the three methods of deduction, induction, and language analysis. The truth of a matter is always tentative, adjudicated by our experiences and reasoning ability.

Infinities

Let us use our reason to examine the conundrum of the tortoise and the hare. The infinite regression is a construct that is basic to differential and integral calculus, fundamental methods of advanced mathematics and modern physics. The principles involved are deductive and involve the concept of a limit. Comparing speed to velocity, Newton and Leibniz arrived at the notion of instantaneous velocity as opposed to average velocity or speed. Average velocity is calculated by dividing the differences of distance covered by the time consumed. The instantaneous velocity, or the differential of distance by time, is this ratio as the distance and time approach zero.

It was a revolutionary concept. Newtonian mechanics of velocity, acceleration, and force all depend upon differential calculus. Likewise, current theories of energy fields, quantum mechanics, and general relativity rely on these notions. All of these theories employ infinities, which is implied by the concept of a limit. One can see the similarity to the infinite halving of distances in our fable.

These infinities are anathema to our common sense, which does not believe there can be an infinite (unlimited) distance between the tortoise and hare. Rather our consciousness perceives things as a continuous phenomenon over stretches of time, in the Bergsonian sense (30).

Difficulties involving infinities arise in other areas. Multiple infinities are encountered in explaining the Brownian motion of gas molecules in an enclosed space. By some theories each molecule has an infinite possibility for each spatial and time dimension (four infinities). Infinities on top of infinities.

Similar infinities are seen when applied to maps. Boundaries, such as those between land and water, are perceived differently depending upon the scale. As the scale is magnified, new intricacies are identified although there does seem to be some similarity among the different scales (31). Presumably, there could be an infinite array of different scales.

Many components of nature are not easily amenable to scientific scrutiny. They behave chaotically, such as the apparent random activity of fluids, why eddies form, the prediction of weather, and when the next stock market crash will ensue. Small changes at a distant site might produce major changes in the future, the so-called "butterfly effect" (31). However, with our common sense, we have no difficulty accepting chaotic behavior with non-linear randomness.

Additionally, discrepancies occur between common-sense and scientific depictions. Newtonian physics is couched in idealized situations. For example, inertial systems are unchanging in the idealized circumstance, unless they are acted upon by another force, such as friction. But we are not in a frictionless world, so the common-sense view is more to the point. However, the idealized system allows us to express mathematically the dynamics of force. It is our reasoning capacity that allows us to explain why and how the different presentations are clarified.

Returning to the tortoise and hare example, we can use a concept derived from quantum mechanical theory to resolve the controversy. At the end of the nineteenth century, Max Planck theorized that the energy of a wave function is related to its frequency (the number of vibrations per unit of time) by a set constant, which has been named Planck's constant. Instead of the energy being a continuous function (with infinite regressions), it is packaged in discrete amounts or quanta. This relates the wave function to the particulate nature of light, basic to quantum mechanics (10).

Further, Einstein's brilliant relativity theories relate the mass of a particle to its energy (E=mass times the square of the speed of light) (10). In energy field theory, spatial and time quantities are expressed as vectors, which include discrete amounts, related to Planck's constant. All of these variables, then, are in discrete bundles of Planck's constant, including time and space (10). Although the continuous, infinite regressions are useful mathematical constructs, they do not represent reality in its most basic manner. Length, time, mass, energy, velocity, and acceleration occur only in discrete amounts.

Mr. Tortoise was incorrect in his claim that he could not be beaten. The claim was obviously unfounded by common-sense reasoning. It was also not confirmed by empirical observation. Had Mr. Tortoise studied his physics syllabus more carefully, he never would have made such an obvious error.

SECTION III. MORALITY.
HOW SHOULD WE LIVE?

How we should live is perhaps our most important philosophical question. It is discussed in detail in the large essay published in my first book of philosophical essays, which is included here as Essay 9 (1). It has been modified slightly, mostly in style. How to lead a good life is complex, as each of us knows. The contention here is that it has to be navigated among five life challenges: our health; our work, broadly characterized; morality; political expression; and esthetic and religious notions. It is argued that there are conflicts among these categories.

Morality is presented as a desire to advance some leveling of inequalities among us by restricting liberties. The rationale for this is related to our natural freedom being juxtaposed against our moral sense. Our moral mission to promote some equality comes at the cost of restricting liberties. Its political implementation balances liberty with equality.

Essays 10 and 11 deal with two moral issues, lying and racism.

It is evident that our nature, as discussed in the first 6 essays, and how we think in Essays 7 and 8, relate critically to how we should live our lives.

Essay 9. The Good Life

Introduction

The ancient Greeks, especially Plato and Aristotle, used the term "happiness" synonymously with the "Good Life," but this is too simplistic, even if happiness is defined more broadly as well-being. It suggests that their Good Life is something akin to pleasure, which is far too frivolous for our complex nature. The Good Life is difficult to describe in terms of set prescriptions and proscriptions, as there are often contesting tenets depending upon the point of view. This is not to say that morality is always "subjective"; rather it asserts that making normative judgments is difficult. Socrates and Aristotle felt that our lives should be conjoined with the most characteristic feature of our species, our intellectual, thinking capacity. But does this apply equally to those who are less intelligent or those who are barely eking out an existence?

Jesus and Paul preached that all the necessities of life would be provided to those with sufficient faith in God. But what if food, shelter, and water are not provided in a famine? Jesus and Paul also promulgated complete egalitarianism, an expression of loving one's neighbor as oneself. However, aren't there gradations of love? If all love were equal, would the concept of love somehow be cheapened? Is my love for my newborn child different from my love for a stranger or for God? If all things are shared equally, who produces the goods that are to be shared? These examples are problematic, as obvious conflicts are evident.

This essay is an approach to these problems, which elucidates their difficulties. Even the concept of the Good Life is difficult to define, as it must differ depending upon the importance of each category for each individual at his stage in life. The five major categories of this discussion are: (1) The maintenance of one's health; (2) The need for "work," broadly defined, to fulfill our biologic needs; (3) Moral or ethical considerations; (4) Political implementation; and (5) The esthetic category, including many religious practices and tenets. The examples provided show necessary tensions among these categories, depending upon existential circumstances. The discussion relies heavily upon the importance of the situation at hand and human nature. The cited examples include human experiences of daily life, literature, philosophy, science, and the arts.

In this deliberation it is assumed from the outset that we are naturally reasonable and that we have a moral sense. Otherwise, it would be senseless to have any persuasive discourse. One cannot use reason to prove reasonableness. Also, it is impossible to have an ethical controversy unless there is a moral sense upon which actions can be judged. Our moral sense is evident in feelings of compassion and altruism, sometimes resulting in charity, promoting equality. The moral sense is also seen in the converse when we experience shame or guilt for our immoral behavior. We will not all come to the same moral conclusions, as these questions are often complex and nuanced, but the moral process is the same.

Some cultures with different socio-religious doctrines might come to moral conclusions different from those in Western civilizations, especially with regard to dicta regarding behavior that does not obviously produce harm. The food proscriptions, canons of some religions, might provide bases for reasons for one's action or moral sense. These food dicta are generally not universal. However, the process of doing an action for a reason, justifying the action, is present in each of us. Although most might not accept the reason for the action, the rational and moral thinking are always present.

The moral sense is innate, although it relies on rationality. The moral capacity grows with rational maturity. The moral sense is clearer when harm to another might ensue. For example, all things being equal, we understand that a bully should not take a lollipop from a young, innocent child.

Both freedom and a moral sense are components of our nature and sometimes work at cross-purposes. These aspects of our nature are explored in detail in the sections on work, morality, and political implementation.

Reliance on other aspects of our nature is also embodied in this essay. Although there may be some controversy regarding the genetic and environmental mix in their genesis, most reasonable people agree to their presence. We learn early in life that there is an external world, its characteristics being supported by the complementarities of our senses. This world is enmeshed in time and space.

Part of the world is our body; we are a biologic species, with physiologic needs. We are also an imperfect species, with a limited life span, and with many frailties. We are mortal, and each day may be our last. There are significant inequalities among us, especially regarding aspects that improve our ability to get on through our lives.

We consist of two genders that are strikingly different. Interactions between the genders comprise much of the stuff of morality. We are also social beings, exemplified by our use of language, which is the vehicle of our thought's expression, and necessarily requires other people. This social context is the subject of the fourth category, political implementation.

Finally, we also have an esthetic and religious sense, which is quite variable among us, and is explored in the final section.

Some modern philosophers have suggested that the considerations of this essay are outside of the sphere of philosophy, and that philosophic inquiry might best be suited for analysis of meaning and language. For this essay, it is assumed that our nature is far more complex and that moral, political, religious and esthetic considerations are also open to analysis. Ludwig Wittgenstein suggested that the more interesting aspects of our cognitive life are in the areas outside of his pioneering, modern philosophy (32). This essay relates the above-enumerated aspects of our nature to a conception of the Good Life. Life is a process and each of our lives should be viewed accordingly. Our navigating this process involves important choices for which we are responsible. Conflicts among the five categories outlined show some of the difficulties encountered in this process.

Health Issues

The maintenance of one's health has to be our first priority, as one is restricted without a healthy body. We are a fragile species, imperfect in many ways, necessitating this need to keep us functional. Our lives are often fraught with suffering, both physically and emotionally. Further, we are an unequal species, with these burdens shared disproportionately. As discussed in the following section, our work, broadly stated, deals with these problems. Support of our family's and our suffering and disabilities is a major charge of our work.

One's health is much more important for older individuals whose health problems are more common. Often, fulfilling the daily issues with one's health comprises a large component of one's efforts, particularly with the degenerative aspects of aging. The young can also be struck with chronic illnesses such as diabetes mellitus, cancer, inflammatory bowel disease, drug and alcohol addiction, and psychiatric illness that can be potentially as debilitating as the diseases of the aging population.

A careful examination of our individual frailties, including the alteration of our moods, the effect of circadian rhythms in our daily lives and perceptions, the effects of our environment, our individual susceptibilities to aberrant emotional reactions, including our predisposition to depression, all play a role in maintaining our health. Each of us should be aware of a familial predisposition to obesity, heart disease, alcoholism, drug abuse, and some cancers, and should act accordingly with appropriate medical screening and dietary management.

Establishing routines and rituals can be important in combating these tendencies. These are particularly important in the elderly and disabled in whom the activities of daily living consume large amounts of their daily life. They include regular exercise; avoidance of obesity, excessive alcohol, cigarettes, and illicit drugs; regular physician visits, immunizations, and screening; compliance with prescribed medications; and attention to excretory and other bodily functions.

One of the facts of life relates to fate, fortune, and our mortality. Various approaches to this reality have been advocated to deal with these facts of our existence. We might suddenly contract a fatal, incurable illness or be maimed in an accident. A brilliant mind might be stuck with Alzheimer's dementia. Your youngest child might develop childhood leukemia. Religious traditions have fostered approaches. Also, many superstitions have been built on preventing or predicting these eventualities. The stoic or Epicurean approach might be the most beneficial, encouraging us to move forward, expending our remaining years in the most fruitful ways, regardless of the circumstances of fate, accepting those things that are out of our control, and dealing predominantly with those within our control.

Although the loss of a loved one or of an important physical function can be overwhelming, the measure of one's self is how he deals with these things. This is not to belittle the very human emotions of grief, resentment, and anger that attend these realities. In truth, the dispassionate approach alone does not allow for the poignant expression of our human feelings. Avoidance of these potential feelings does not allow for living life as fully as possible. Some of the noblest human emotional expressions are seen with the loss of a loved one.

The daily activities with health in some individuals may eclipse or come into conflict with the other four categories. For example, a young man responsible for supporting his family and himself financially for their basic and more extended needs could compromise his health. He might decide to postpone necessary surgery to fulfill this function. On the other hand, he might decide that his health needs take priority in spite of his financial obligations. This requirement for gainful employment is discussed in the next section.

There are additional conflicting issues. Our moral nature strives for equality of increased access for health care, but conflicts arise with the need for taxation of the wealthier to support the less advantaged. Finally, religious and moral considerations arise with abortion, embryonic stem cell research and therapy, and cloning, among others.

Work, Gainful Employment

Gainful employment is a component of the Good Life. As biologic entities we have basic needs including food, water, shelter, and clothing; and other more expansive needs of love, sex, family, and self-esteem. Work, broadly defined, allows us to fulfill these needs, but it differs for each individual. Most of these needs may be available to someone who inherits wealth, whose major work challenge is the gratification of his feelings of self-esteem, perhaps through avocations. On the other hand, hunter-gatherers, scratching out subsistence in the tundra, spent most of their time and effort on basic survival. Aggressive aspects of our nature facilitated this quest for survival, and these behavioral aspects have been maintained in modern humans, mostly in men.

Family and clan development expanded these basic needs to include their survival. Competition for resources resulted in clan warfare. Some virtues are components of this process, including physical strength, honor, pride, self-esteem, loyalty, respect for authority, and courage. They strengthen family and community bonds. The expansion of clans to cities, states, and nations has augmented some of these tendencies. Negatively prejudicial feelings toward the "other" have occurred as a consequence.

Warfare has always been with us and is a manifestation of these aggressive qualities. The tempering of these aggressive elements has occurred coincidentally, first by leaders of clans, later by more complex political processes. Concepts of justice have been promulgated, although formulaic dicta have been elusive (discussed below under the political category).

Sex, love, and family are needs, predominantly biologic, often more potent than the needs for survival. A lovesick Juliet will sacrifice her fidelity to her family for Romeo, ignoring the potential harmful consequences (33). Likewise, Natasha Rostov sacrifices her pledge to Andrei Bolkonsky for her infatuated love for Anatole (18). Clearly the fulfillment of romantic love serves a purpose in the fostering of family. In addition, it captures some of the most intense human emotions, described vividly in our literature.

But the biology of romantic, heterosexual love is incompletely expressed in humans, as we are an imperfect or uneven species, evident from the presence of homosexuality, bisexuality, congenital imperfections, and acquired defects. In some, sexual orientation is ambiguous, especially during the formative years as childhood blossoms into adulthood.

Some of the virtues expressed above (physical strength, courage, honor, pride, self-esteem, loyalty) come into significant conflicts with moral, political, and religious considerations. Prudence and humility are often considered moral virtues, but are in contradistinction to courage (especially when foolhardy), honor, and pride. Juliet and Natasha abandon the virtue of fidelity for their perceived greater fidelity. The judgment whether an action is good or evil is difficult when these opposing virtues come into play. Sometimes, simple biologic considerations are paramount. We cannot escape from our biologic realities. Judging the aggressive actions of tribes in sub-Saharan Africa, suffering from limited food and water, with consequent widespread starvation, is complicated. Are killing, stealing, and war ever justified in these circumstances? Are these aggressive actions tempered by rules of conflict, often seen in these struggles?

The importance of our life's work is evident from our spending much of our time and effort in our work. Although it fulfills the biologic needs expressed above, it also allows the potential for developing a sense of purpose, our expressing who each of us is. For some cultures, this development is necessitated by the simple tasks of survival. But, even there, virtues such as bravery, honor, honesty, loyalty, filial bonds, integrity, and leadership can be embraced and can be sources of individual pride and self-esteem. Habits and routines fulfilling of our health needs as outlined in the prior section can be helpful in fostering our work too. Ideally, we should choose a life's work that is "for itself," inner directed, in the J. P. Sartre sense (34).

In some respects, we are less free when fulfilling biologic needs. Emotions such as envy, jealousy, greed, love, and hate arise outside of our conscious control. These emotions are extensions of our biologic needs. For example, envy and greed relate to our need for survival, and jealousy to our need for sex and love. Their fulfillment, even when freely performed, has an element of compulsion. Freedom is best expressed when we do things for a reason, justifying our actions in language. Although slaking one's thirst or hunger is free action, the freedom displayed is qualitatively different from the more complex free actions we perform daily. In addition, there is more of an element of individual responsibility involved in these complex actions.

The freedom to perform our work should be advanced as one of the distinguishing features of our nature and as a primary component of the Good Life. However, conflicts arise when this exercise of our liberty interferes with others'. In general, we should support free expression in all its modes unless the reasons for their suppression are very good. Our freedom is attenuated by our desire for equality, the hallmark of morality, which introduces us to the third category.

Morality

It has been argued that morality is simply hedonism, the avoidance of pain and the seeking of pleasure. However, this ignores the conjunction of some pleasures with their converse pain. It is truly pleasurable following the pain of vigorous exercise. Slaking of thirst and hunger is more pleasurable than the complete absence of both. Seeking pleasure and avoiding pain are clearly natural processes and should be encouraged, so long as they do not interfere with our more important functions. Hedonism ignores the moral sense that we all have. Although there are some with a limited moral sense, often psychopathic, who ignore ethical precepts and embrace hedonism with no compunction, they are unusual and have to learn to conform to the tenets of society to survive.

Most of us deal with choices daily, for which we take responsibility, as freedom and responsibility go hand in hand. We are judged externally and personally by these actions. It is tautological that good behavior, in a moral sense, is a component of the Good Life. It makes no sense to propose that a life imbued with evil actions could be a component of the Good Life, even if it conforms to the pleasure principle. The difficulty is the assessment of the morality of our actions, which may be complicated by opposing virtues. Regardless of the difficulties, it is necessary to state that free action, responsibility, and a moral sense are part of our nature, and attempting to act morally or ethically must be encouraged.

A. The Golden Rule. Many efforts have been made to adduce generalized moral principles, universally held. Problems with the application of most of these principles are evident. Kant's categorical imperative, and Jesus' and Paul's golden rule are examples. They advocate that the morality of an action on another is best judged by putting oneself in the other's position. Would I want to be treated in the way that I intend to treat the other? This moral principle seems simple enough, and most believe the world would be better if it were more frequently observed. However, it is very difficult to enact in our daily lives, perhaps related to the biologic needs expressed above. For example, the need to provide for shelter, food, and clothing for our immediate family and us is biologic, required for our family's, and our, survival. This need may supersede the general moral principle.

Others might suffer from the fulfillment of this competitive spirit. The capitalistic outlook and Social Darwinism are consequences, which can be viewed as good, as our own survival may trump potential ethical conflicts. Property, power over other people, and wealth become components of this process, and some of the virtues of industriousness, pride, and augmented self-esteem result. Political liberty, with no external constraints, is its ultimate expression, but can result in untoward consequences. Acquisitiveness can become extreme, with the accumulation of wealth far exceeding these biologic needs.

Kant's and Jesus' dictum promotes a leveling or equalizing process. Our senses of empathy and sympathy, resulting in charitable feelings or actions, reflect this tendency, regardless of the clan, skin color, nation or background. In general this approach is morally sound. But there is a tension between unbridled liberty and equality. The golden rule could then be employed individually to temper excessive liberty. Although freedom is a component of our nature and should be fostered, one can see that it can infringe on others' freedoms. Neither excessive liberty nor excessive equality by itself should be components of the Good Life. Rather, both should be involved, modified by the specific life situation.

B. Killing. The 10 Commandments likewise are reasonable moral canons. Leaving aside the religious commandments for now, we can look at the remainder. The commandment not to kill is recognized by most cultures, but they make exceptions. Survival of individuals, groups, and nations can depend upon hostile competition, which can result in death and may trump the proscription against killing. War seems to be a part of our nature, the ultimate expression of this competition. The Jews of the Bible describe many wars that included deaths that were accepted. Many believe that World War II was a just war, morally warranted, in spite of the loss of over 40 million people.

Although Socrates generally felt that taking another's life was unjust, he did participate as a Hoplite warrior for Athens. Further, he accepted his own death, as the political process of Athens, the city he loved, sentenced it. Supporting the political process supervened his aversion to his homicide, even though the sentencing was wrong.

Suicide is likewise very complex. Do others ever have the moral right to condemn or restrict this ultimate freedom from anyone? And, yet, it is reasonable to prevent suicide when attempted for magical reasons in the mentally ill.

C. Lying, Stealing, Coveting. The proscription against bearing false witness is considered an ideal for most. Being truthful is one of the measures of an honorable individual. If one is not truthful, how can he be trusted? However, it is problematic in some circumstances. The commonly cited example of the Nazis asking if any Jews are hidden in the attic is telling. Lying under this circumstance seems appropriate. What is the difference between hiding truth from someone and speaking an untruth? Must we always open our hearts and minds to others? Is lying or hiding truth acceptable if it protects someone else and does not benefit the liar? These questions are difficult to answer for all situations.

Lying in some sense is stealing from others, robbing the truth. Cheating is a combination of stealing and lying. Stealing property is considered unlawful in most societies, supporting the concept of property rights. However, exceptions can be seen. Would it be right to steal someone's slave so that the slave could be released from bondage? On the other side of the coin, is taxation an enforced method of stealing, a method for leveling wealth among all people? This issue will be discussed further in the political implementation section.

Coveting or desiring others' property (in Exodus, another's wife or ass) is an extension of stealing, as it precedes, or is the inducement for, stealing. Is the desire for others' property or the feeling of envy immoral in itself? Envy that is not implemented in action is clearly internal, not available for analysis by other people. In addition, it arises naturally, usually without voluntary control, similar to other feelings or sensations (hate, love, empathy, sympathy, thirst, hunger, chill, warmth, pain). It is an accompaniment or a consequence of the very basic need for survival, discussed above, which eclipses moral considerations in some circumstances (starving tribes in sub-Saharan Africa). One can temper these feelings, but eliminating them may be impossible, as they are a part of our nature.

As for other moral tenets, interpretation of an action is complex, sometimes requiring an in-depth study of each alternative and its consequences. The facts include knowing the entire story of the people involved, including motives, in the C. S. Lewis sense (35). Perhaps the bully who took the lollipop was protecting the diabetic child, his sister, from the untoward effects of too much sugar.

D. Male-female Interactions. Perhaps the most prominent moral complexity is seen in male-female interactions. There is a curiosity about the other gender, seen early in childhood, and continuing into adulthood. In addition, there is a tendency to display each of us favorably to the other gender. This blossoms with sexual development in adolescence, resulting in the most potent emotional feelings that we experience. Romantic love can displace rationality, overwhelming individuals, as with Juliet and Natasha, described above. In the desire for the beloved, one might ignore the needs for shelter, food, water, and work. Its satisfaction becomes predominant. In general, the stronger male overcomes the initial reluctance of the compliant female in consummating this love.

This biology comes into play with some of the aberrations evident in modern society. Pornography, voyeurism, and indecent exposure are exaggerated expressions of this curiosity and the reciprocal enticing of the observed. Rape, prostitution, and sex slavery are the most sordid examples. It is understandable that society and institutions have instigated moral dicta, laws, and unwritten rules governing conduct between the sexes. Most of these rules are to protect the female from the aggressive, stronger male, and to foster the healthy environment for family cohesiveness and growth, which most agree is morally sound. Implementation can be extreme, as in some Muslim traditions, keeping the female covered and unexposed to the male, except to family members. The Victorian rules for polite interaction between the sexes were similarly extreme.

Rules for the morality of sexual intercourse are not invariably held. The Hebrew commandment against adultery is not universally accepted. Abraham, the father of monotheism, had two wives. Islam and Mormonism have allowed multiple wives. The modern Western tradition has, for the most part, accepted the approach of mutual consent being the overriding principle defining the moral and legal standings of this most intimate relationship.

However, how does one decide consent in this emotionally charged process? Doesn't consent depend upon the mindset or internal thoughts that one has during the event? How much rational decision making is involved in sexual intercourse when it is predominantly a biologic process? When is consent given – at the time of consummation or as early as agreeing to have any intimate interaction in the absence of a chaperone? Is there support for moral repugnancy for someone who brags of his thousands of sexual conquests, even with mutual consent? Is there no qualitative moral difference between sexual intercourse and other biologic processes such as urination or defecation? Is prostitution always immoral, even when it is the only option for survival for a woman and her child? It seems as if the survival instinct would supersede the moral in this circumstance. Is there a difference between

Emma Bovary's sexual exploits and Dr. Zhivago's? (36). Dr. Zhivago's actions appear to be more acceptable, morally, as his involvement with Lara seemed unique, and resulted from events mostly out of his control.

The biologic need for love and sexual gratification are profound expressions of our nature. They ought to be expressed in this light. Although Crazy Jane might expound that love is in the place of excrement, one more enlightened realizes that love and sex are personal, private, and of utmost importance in our lives (37). These aspects of our nature can be cheapened by bizarre aberrations, but the aberrations miss the point. Truly loving another puts each lover on an equal footing, each desiring satisfaction of the other as much as their self. Using another simply as a means to a selfish end demeans each participant.

A natural consequence of male-female interaction is pregnancy, eventuating in offspring. The natural sequence of pregnancy and parenting cannot be taken lightly, as it is one of our most important human processes. This consequence should be borne by both parents, during the gestation process and subsequently with the child's birth. Each ought to assume responsibility for the rearing of the child and to provide their loving, caring interest. The child should respect and love his parents, supporting the development of family, another natural result.

Decisions on indiscriminate sexual activity, contraception, abortion, marriage, and divorce should not be taken lightly as they affect not only the coupling but also the potential or actual reality of a separate, unique human. Much of our moral and religious considerations revolve around this eventuality.

The complexities of inter-gender morality are more obscure with other aspects of modern life. Is self-exposure to another over the Internet immoral or is it simply modern courting? Are some of the verbal innuendoes between the sexes in the workplace normal interchange or are they sexual harassment? Was it morally justifiable to claim sexual harassment when Clarence Thomas was undergoing his Supreme Court confirmation, nearly impossible to prove, contingent upon verbal recollection and knowing the intent within another's mind (38)? When does the biologic, aggressive, masculine aspect of the sex drive morph into immoral activity?

In many respects, the moral issues between the genders were much more easily adjudicated within the Muslim and Victorian traditions than in our modern secular societies, both recognizing the biologic potency between the sexes. Clearly, extreme circumstances such as forcible rape must be abhorred, and the weaker female should be provided with some protection from the potential aggressive actions of the male. However, there are intermediary situations where the morality is not very clear.

The inclination of the stronger male to protect his mate and his family is part of our nature, is morally sound and should be promulgated. The inherent complexity of morality between the sexes should not deter one from affirming its unmistaken importance. The overwhelming experience of the loving activity, culminating in marriage and blossoming in children and grandchildren are unlike any other process. The natural relation of mother and child both in the womb and after can be all-consuming for both. The Judeo-Christian tradition supporting the sanctity of marriage supports this natural tendency. The weaker female should accept this arrangement with her expressed, monogamous relationship. The father naturally should be the protector of mother, child, and eventually family, as his personal responsibility. The role of grandparents is subtler, but the strong emotional bond to children and grandchildren is also part of our nature. We should support and foster all of these human institutions.

D. Homosexuality. Pedophilia. On the other hand, we are an imperfect species, and all are not capable of this heterosexual love, its consummation, and the development of a family. By environment or genetics, some have homosexual preference, precluding this ultimate expression. In addition, many have acquired or inborn defects preventing this fulfillment. Their lives will involve other activities.

There are also aberrant sexual preferences, such as pedophilia. How we relate to these practices and deficiencies that are out of the mainstream is an important moral question. It seems that tolerance and respect for those different would be morally prudent. However, those with these aberrant predilections must not be allowed to act out their desires. They have to realize that their lives require enjoining these practices.

This is not to say that the life of those with sexual preferences outside of the mainstream, or those physically or emotionally impaired, cannot have a full life. Rather, it is to say that their lives are different. For example, a pedophile's predilections preclude intimate involvement with children. However, the impulses can be channeled or sublimated into his being an advocate for children. This eventuality might be considered heroic.

Further, many of us have less pronounced sociopathy or psychopathy that requires therapy, suppression or sublimation. Similarly, a homosexual cannot share in heterosexual experiences, genetic family, children, and grandchildren, but he can have a loving homosexual relationship as a component of his life. Heterosexuals should respect and encourage this loving relationship, which is fulfilling, unlike promiscuous "hooking up" behavior that might otherwise occur.

E. Equality and Liberty. Limitations of power are also morally sound in relationships with others in a dependent position, such as with employer/employee situations, with lower animals, and with the world. The tyrannical use of power in any of these circumstances is harmful not only to the powerless entity, but also to the tyrant. For example, someone in power should not use it to induce sexual relations in a dependent individual. Although beasts of burden should be employed when necessary, they should be treated kindly and with respect, and should not simply be considered property. We should limit our liberty to spoil the environment, and should strive to make our beautiful world as good or better for the next generation.

Most moral behavior is viewed in terms of its effect on other people and its impact on the freedom of others. In a sense, our moral nature is a modifying influence on our own liberty. When one's freedom unjustly infringes upon the freedom of others, ethical considerations come into play.

Babies and young children have much less moral sense than adults, as evident from the necessity to enforce rules of behavior by parents, grandparents, and teachers. Whenever restrictions are posed, the authority figures have to be cognizant of the detrimental effects of too much restriction of the children's individual liberty.

Many of these moral tenets manifest charity, a respect for others and the practice of helping others in need. With few exceptions, charity is a component of the Good Life. Charitable contributions can be as simple as respecting another's point of view or religion, or as complex as establishing a charitable organization. Much of what we consider virtuous behavior can be subsumed under the charitable category. Charitable acts benefit not only the recipient, but also the donor.

F. Morality Involving Customs. Morality involving customs that do not obviously cause harm to another raises additional complexities. Is it immoral for someone to be impolite to another in modern society? Harm can result with bruised feelings. Pushing this further, should behavior be enjoined if one does not have the appropriate manners during a social interchange? How should one behave regarding food proscriptions that are not shared when dining with another? How ought one discuss significantly different principles among different faiths? In all of these circumstances, the best approach is to respect the "other," realizing that there are significant differences among us. This is not to say that everyone ought to be treated equally. It would be unnatural for a father to deal with a stranger in the same way as he deals with his son. However, promoting comity within our species is a noble goal.

G. Complexity of Morality. An example. An example of how moral considerations can be used in looking at a specific circumstance can be instructive. Jonathan Haidt presented a vignette from his own life in his book on moral psychology, which helped him in developing his concept on the distinction between innate morality and reasoning (39). After he left dirty dishes on the counter, his wife scolded him. He responded quickly with excuses, justifying his neglect. Later, upon reflection, he realized that he lied to his wife, as the reasons given for his inaction were untrue. He expanded this example in developing his major thesis, that thinking (rationalizing, language, explaining) serves innate notions of morality, rather than develops them.

This story can be analyzed on many different levels. First is a discussion of the real reason for not following the family rule. He may have been preoccupied with his writing of his moral psychology essay, which took precedence over the rule. He may simply have forgotten, as "absentminded professors" might. He also might have objected to the rule, and a better rule would be that anyone could leave out dirty dishes, although the rule was instituted because of a need to have a clean space to prepare the baby's food. Down deep, he may have thought that the rule was beneath him. Regardless, the reasons that he gave were excuses and were untrue. He lied to his wife. He did not "own up."

The second level is the reason for lying to his wife. The obvious one is that he wanted to cover up his negligence. The answer is solely known to him, as no one can read another's mind. The reasons given for an action may be true or false, but only the actor knows for sure.

The third level relates to the principle that the rapid reasoning process was supposed to have supported his innate moral beliefs. Was it the rule itself that was innate? The rule that he should not have been disturbed by his nagging wife? The rule that only some have to obey rules? These sound silly because they are. All of those "rules" are evanescent and are not innate. The innate function is the moral reasoning capacity that humans have, which is demonstrated in these seven paragraphs.

The fourth level relates to the subtle notion advanced that somehow rationalizations occur so suddenly that we have no control or responsibility. We are responsible for our actions as we are free. It is true that we have little control over our feelings and emotions, as they passively enter our consciousness. But we have the responsibility for how we respond to the emotions.

At a final level, the author of this essay, married to the same wife for 50 years, offers the following suggestion: "You are right, dear, and I shall try to modify my behavior in the future. It is ironic that I was working on a moral psychology paper and did not observe our rule that was made to protect our baby. I'll try to improve; please forgive me." His wife would immediately recognize his humanity, forgive him, know he was telling the truth, and love him more.

This analysis relates to Aristotle's dictum that a moral person is one who practices moral behavior and becomes that moral person.

H. Concluding Statements on Morality. The above considerations outline the complexities of morality, often clouded by opposing opinions, ideals, or virtues. Examples have been provided in which killing, stealing, lying, and adultery might be justifiable in some circumstances. Trying to determine justice can be difficult due to these opposing forces or tensions. Most of these ensue due to competing tendencies within us and others (biologic processes versus classic morality; liberty versus equality; individual property rights versus charity and caring for others). In some respects morality can be considered an aspect of our nature that balances the natural requirements for survival. Empathy and altruism are expressions of this moral nature, blossoming in egalitarianism. In addition, some of the virtues that evolve from the requirements for survival, including pride and honor, temper the unrestricted use of power. It should be clear that a balancing of unrestricted liberty with our moral sense is required, although formulaic solutions are not evident. However, it is clear that the human mental capacity and our innate moral sense are available in these circumstances.

In the pursuit of the Good Life, individuals, then, have to contend with their health issues first, as one can do little else with poor health. Next, our life's work must be pursued to provide for our basic and more complex needs. The needs are predominantly biologic and can sometimes be overwhelming, bringing conflicts between their satisfaction and moral issues. We should strive to understand who each of us is, including our biologic needs, and resolve the conflicts between their satisfaction and moral understanding. This resolution is often nuanced and not easily accomplished. Unrestricted power and freedom over others should be balanced by the moral tenet of respect for all humans. Absolute freedom should be balanced by feelings of charity, expressed through expanding equality.

Tyrannical bullying of the weaker, women, children, or those less fortunate should be discouraged. Respect for others should be enhanced, and their differences appreciated. Yet some of the characteristics of unrestricted freedom should be celebrated, including pride in one's work, honor, and self-esteem. The unabashed freedoms to kill, lie, and steal should be enjoined, except for unusual circumstances, as the examples outlined above. The complex relationships between the sexes should be dealt with mutual respect, realizing the potency of the natural processes entailed.

Our capacity to fail in our moral tempering of our own liberty for the good of others and ourselves is profound; dealing with this is one of the major problems in our pursuit of the Good Life. Part of our nature is to fail quite miserably with most of these ethical constructs, which some have suggested is related to our "fallen nature," our capacity for sin. As discussed in the section on work and biologic needs, these actions stem from a corruption of our biologic needs into envy, jealousy, greed, and hate.

Some of our most profound human expressions result from the shame or guilt derived from our failing to behave ethically. This should not dissuade us from striving for improvement, and that we should be measured in terms of process rather than end points. We should have a mutual understanding of and empathy for this "fallen nature."

From a personal standpoint, then, depending upon existential circumstances, pursuance of the Good Life sometimes requires maximal expression of our freedom for fulfillment of our health and other biologic needs. In general, our own liberty should be promulgated, restricted only for very good reasons. Most moral actions can be related to avoiding harm to others, but our moral sense also includes altruism, charity, respect for others, and a quest for equality among us. Our liberty and equality come into conflict when our liberty restricts the liberty of others. Our moral sense fostering equality serves as a leveling influence on unrestricted liberty.

Political Implementation

These principles for the individual should be extended to the polis. We are social or political beings, manifested by our use of language, a social instrument. Good politics reflect what is good individually. An understanding of our individual nature is the basis for the good of the polis.

We have strong survival needs, evident in some of our virtues (pride, self-esteem, honor, bravery), but also in some disreputable features, such as avarice, envy, and selfishness, and can result in killing, stealing, lying, and the uncontrolled exercise of tyrannical power. Our nature also is intrinsically ethical, reflecting our rationality, and providing a moral sense that permits normative discourse. Our ethical nature often plays a role in tempering the exercise of those aspects of our nature involved in fulfillment of the basic and secondary needs of our kin and us.

Similar to our own behavior, regulation of the moral and survival aspects of our nature play out in resolution of the tensions between liberty and equality politically. Unrestricted liberty can result in harm to others (loss of property, physical damage, death, slavery). Unrestricted equality can result in loss of property rights, restriction of the entrepreneurial spirit, excessive taxation, and too much regulation of one's freedom. Political solutions have been devised to balance liberty and equality. In some respects, this can be viewed as a process for determining justice for citizens.

In early societies, political decisions were left to the leader of the family, clan, or community. The leader was usually mature and was perceived to be wise. The feudal societies in Europe, and the tribal societies in Africa and the Far East maintained this tradition. Often the leader would be imbued with religious power, further substantiating his authority. This authoritarian government flourished as societies became more advanced with kings and queens having power over large realms, often considered to be connected to a deity.

Plato felt that a Philosopher King would be the best type of ruler, so long as he is imbued with the wisdom of what is good for the populace. This individual would be best suited to judge, in a Solomon-like manner. Although there have been some benign dictators throughout history, such as Marcus Aurelius, most have abused their power restricting both liberty and equality. The problem with Plato's Philosopher King is in the process of choosing one. The horrors from the dictators of the twentieth century attest to this eventuality.

Many of the authoritarian governments throughout history have been theocracies, with the central leader or leaders imbued with a direct relation to the religious order of the community or nation. That system of justice is based on the fundamental belief structure of the stated religion. However, theocracies run the risk of all dictatorial governments, the tyrannical abuse of power for personal benefit.

Some liberties can be supported as rights of the populace that cannot be broached by the state (expanding equality for the populace by restricting liberty of the state). Recognizing that any government can interfere with an individual's free exercise of his rights, the authors of the Bill of Rights of the United States Constitution guaranteed these liberties. In spite of the pontification of these Founding Fathers, it should be clear that we are not created equally. Some have been born with many of the salutary attributes that allow ease in getting on in the world. Some have little of these attributes. Our moralistic, altruistic nature strives to level this playing field. The liberties of the privileged are restricted as equality is expanded. Individuals within the society are treated equally under the law.

Democratic systems of justice were instituted to enforce the expansion of equality. Taxation became necessary to fund the process. Methods for the prevention of other states from usurping these rights were fostered, including the potentiality of war. A balancing of power among different branches of government was developed. Similar systems have been established in other democratic states, which have exemplified the rational distribution of sufficient liberty and equality for all. Most democracies have a representative government, a republic, with the decisions resting on the individuals' representatives.

Systems of justice should balance these ideals, which are often in opposition. Although free speech should be supported, it might have to be restricted if it produces harm. One should be restricted from slandering another publicly or from yelling "fire" in a theater. Taxation of the rich to benefit the poor has to be balanced with ideals of free enterprise, which include self-esteem, pride in one's work, and industriousness. In addition, taxation is a type of theft, taking from one group (the working group) and giving to the governing agencies and to others, presumably less fortunate. Too much redistribution of wealth can inhibit the same industriousness that produces it. It also may inhibit charitable contributions, which can be an unintended result. In general, charitable giving is much more fruitful (benefiting both the donor and the recipient), than forced charity through taxation, which really is no longer charity.

In this process, foolish restrictions of liberty in the quest for equality ought to be avoided. For example, legally eliminating father-daughter dances, because there are some daughters without a father, unduly restricts the liberty of the fathers and daughters.

Proper attention to human biology should enter into rule-making and laws. Although protection of the weak is a lofty goal, laws promulgating equality of the sexes can yield unintended consequences. The deterioration of the family in secular societies might be ascribed to fostering cultural changes over the biologic differences between the genders.

The complexities of tort law demonstrate the difficulties in sorting out this balance. Although someone might have the right to protect himself from harm, when does this process become excessive? Is it necessarily excessive if loss of life results? Likewise, our adjudicated punishments for torts or other illegalities have to be balanced. Is death to another ever morally just? Although Socrates was able to delineate many distinctions in exploring virtues in his dialogues, his discussions of justice are not as definitive. Justice has to be balanced among contrasting virtues.

Politics should maximize liberty, so long as it is not done at the expense of others. Equality should be promulgated as a check on liberty, and should also promote some of the egalitarian aspects of our nature – protecting the weak, unfortunate, and innocent – so long as the expansion does not unduly restrict freedom. One can see that a balance needs to be struck between these contrasting elements.

Finally, it is necessary to see how we should deal with war, which has always been with us, and is a part of our nature, our desire for survival. War is fought predominantly by men and not women, and is a consequence of the nature of men to provide basic needs for themselves and their family. This natural state is expanded to the province of clans, cities, and states, with the unfortunate result in wars. What should the obligation of the state be with this critical issue? Should the state provide for sufficient offensive and defensive weapons potentially to discourage or prevent hostile actions from others? Is it ever justified to initiate a war that is perceived to be inevitable, by a preemptive attack on another state? It would seem that this would encourage too much warfare.

Is any war justifiable? Most would agree that the response of the allies to the attacks of the axis forces in World War II was justifiable, yet World War I was unnecessary and foolish. Wars in the twentieth century were much more devastating to society than those in previous centuries, and the advent of nuclear weapons raises the possibility of our extermination. We should support systems of government that minimize warfare while balancing the requirement to protect against infamy.

Religious, Esthetic, Intellectual Development

Assuming we have cared for our health, have provided for our basic and broader needs, are striving to balance our aggressive with our moralistic, ethical natures, and are living in a society that promotes liberty balanced with equality, we can spend the time and energy developing those additional human concerns, which in many respects reflect our distinctive humanity above all other considerations. These activities can become the most fulfilling and time-intensive aspects of one's life. Someone born healthy, with a suitable inheritance that precludes the necessity of gainful employment, will still have moral challenges, but his major problem to overcome is that of boredom and a lack of structure to his life. Some dissipate into debauchery or drug abuse as an escape from their state. Yet one does have the potential to devote more time to various interests that become the major component of his fulfillment.

On the other hand, a farmer who has to work long hours to provide for himself and his family might have little time for esthetic interests, beyond his religious obligations. He might also find some of the esthetic practices frivolous and not worthy of his attention. A homemaker raising her five children might have little time for esthetic interests, finding meaning in work. Similarly, someone with a disabling physical condition might have to spend all of his time dealing with the activities of daily living, and have little time for these extraneous interests. They might find fulfillment by these daily activities.

A. Religious. For most of us there is a significant religious component to our lives. For Abraham, Moses, Jesus, Saint Paul, Mohammed, Buddha, Kierkegaard, and Mother Teresa, the religious component was all-encompassing. The major risk for these and similar individuals is the potential intolerance of others with different beliefs. From a moral standpoint, religious tolerance should be advanced.

History is replete with examples of immoral disregard for the rights of others' religious beliefs, which has led to atrocities and war. Theocratic societies expressed this intolerance in the Christian Crusades and the countering Islamic militaristic spread of Islam. The persecution of Christian Catholics by Protestants and vice versa in pre-democratic Europe led appropriately to the separation of religion from the state, evident in modern democratic institutions. This separation has supported morality through the respect for others and their beliefs.

Most political institutions have imbued the political entity in power with religious connotations. Early leaders of clans and tribes often had their power substantiated by a relationship with the deity. Theocratic nations have expanded this practice. Democratic constitutions also reinforce their claims by asserting that God endows the rights of man. This practice affirms the natural rights of mankind and our moral nature, although theocratic organizations run the risk of tyranny by overreaching their authority.

Most of us have some religious beliefs, naturally present, that we practice alongside our daily existence. Unlike Jesus, Saint Paul and others, our religious lives are not all-consuming. Our reasoning and moral compass are reflections of our nature, and also point to something above ourselves. The awful joy experienced while listening to the love duet in La Boheme is inspiring. Most of us have difficulty considering our death and non-existence, which is really the death of the world, our world in a Heideggerian sense, for eternity (40). These are religious feelings. Much of literature, poetry, visual arts, music, and other esthetic interests have religion as a predominant element. Our religious feelings are our own, in spite of there being some shared beliefs with others. Some of our human virtues relate directly to religious experience, such as chastity, humility, charity, and prayerfulness.

On the other hand, conflicts can arise between our moral nature and our religion, particularly when dealing with others' religious views. Some of the most poignant human experiences are from others' and our suffering, from physical and emotional disturbance, and from our wrestling with guilt and shame. Religious experience is often a component of adjudicating this process. These religious feelings are uniquely human and should be cherished.

B. Intellectual, Philosophical. Socrates, Aristotle, the stoics, and the Epicureans mostly felt that our highest activity is intellectual. The other activities are involved in our lesser animal makeup, and in many respects should be relegated to a subhuman status. Socrates' dictum that 'the unexamined life is not worth living' is telling. However, it is clear that many do not have the interest or aptitude for in-depth involvement in philosophy or other intellectual disciplines. Having read Heidegger and Wittgenstein, I believe that most of the ontological, epistemic, and linguistic discussions are difficult to comprehend and are not of interest to most. Some other intellectual pursuits including quantum chemistry, nuclear physics, musical theory, twenty-first century orchestral music, and higher mathematics also fit in this mold.

The subjugation of our other esthetic interests to something less than human is misunderstanding our nature. Romantic love can be the most important and poignant experience that we humans have, and should not be relegated simply to an expression of our animalistic appetites.

An appreciation of beauty itself, although hard to define, is wholly human. Much of our esthetic life is engaged in our involvement in love, religion, and these non-intellectual pursuits.

C. Other Esthetic Interests. The involvement in other esthetic interests clearly is individualized, depending upon our individual interests and aptitudes. Our lives can be enriched by involvement in many esthetic activities including sports, music, poetry, literature, visual arts, theater, good food and drink, and social engagements in general. In some, the esthetic interest coincides with one's gainful occupation and work. In others with a strong religious calling, the activity becomes all-encompassing. Regardless, all of these esthetic activities are totally human and should be applauded and encouraged.

Virtues

Socrates often embraced virtuous behavior in his dialogues, and most of us value and recognize virtue. Virtuous action celebrates the dignity of mankind. However, definitions of virtue are often clouded. It should be clear by now that several virtues are often in opposition to other virtues. In addition, virtuous behavior is often best seen when the virtues are tempered. Courage, fostered by our need to provide for and protect us and our family is in contrast to prudence, another virtue. Further, courage must be distinguished from foolhardiness and prudence from cowardice.

The fulfillment of the family's and our basic and extended needs are promoted by courage and honor, but these virtues can be distorted by envy, jealousy, and greed. Pride in one's work, ambition, and ownership of property can be viewed as virtues, so long as they are not perceived as avaricious and self-promoting. In addition, they are tempered by the virtue, humility, expounded by many religious traditions.

Prayerfulness, humility, universal love, and absolute egalitarianism might be viewed as virtuous but might not be seen in the same light if threatened by a tyrannical force promising to destroy, pillage, and rape its society. Further, the virtues of humility, forgiveness, and charity might not be viewed as laudable if they encourage or reward irresponsible behavior. Righteousness is a virtue employed to rectify not to forgive reprehensible actions, and is often the framework for legalistic justification. Loyalty to state, family, religion, and authority are considered virtues, but sometimes might require the courage to oppose the same, when it is behaving tyrannically. Religious cultures supporting the virtues chastity and modesty between the genders can interfere with a woman's freedom if tyrannically enforced.

Of course, justice is played out between the opposing principles or virtues, liberty and equality. The meek, underprivileged, physically or emotionally disabled individuals should be viewed with empathy and caring, but they are not served well by pity. Rather, they are best served by providing opportunity for them to deal with their deficiencies and potentially to act heroically. Our rational and moralistic nature avails itself to sort out these opposing virtues.

Five Overlying Guidelines for the Good Life

1. Take care of your health so that you can get on with your living. This should not be all-consuming, except for exceptional circumstances, and should be a means to an end, not an end in itself.

2. Work is necessary to provide for the basic and secondary needs for you, your family, and your clan. It is a manifestation of your freedom, and allows for maximum expression of many virtues: pride, self-esteem, courage, honor, and loyalty. Its dangers reside in conflicts with your moral nature, wherein fostering equality, charity, and humility might be neglected.

3. Your moral nature obliges you to respect those different from you and those less endowed. It also urges you to protect and respect women, children, other animal species, and our planet. Through your moral nature, you should realize that virtues often need to be balanced among opposing virtues, and between equality and liberty. Acting charitably is almost always a component of the Good Life. Helping others get through the difficulties of living is almost always virtuous. Charity should be considered in an inclusive sense with respect for others, regardless of clan, religion, race or beliefs. We should strive to have our interactions with others civil and polite. Others should be given the benefit of the doubt. Forgiveness is almost always virtuous. Equality should be expanded to the extent that liberty is not unduly restricted, and that the restrictions should not be instituted frivolously.

4. With rare exceptions, we are obliged to respect and honor our polis and be responsible in obeying enacted laws. Participation in good citizenship, including voting, jury duty, and engagement in the political processes are part of the Good Life. Supporting laws that advance equality and do not excessively restrict our freedoms should be encouraged.

5. Finally, the Good Life enjoys its full flowering in religious and esthetic traditions, including the awe inspired by the miracle that each of us is here for a short time.

CONCLUSION

This essay was written to show that there are significant conflicts among these categories of the Good Life, and that a simple formula is not available. The Good life is involved in the maintenance of one's health, gainful employment, the striving to live within our natural sense of morality, in a political institution that fosters both liberty and equality. Navigating our needs against others' challenges our free and moral natures. We are further challenged by our failure to meet these obligations, resulting in shame, guilt and emotional suffering. For some, the obligations of health maintenance, work and moral challenges are so great that little time or inclination is left for esthetic interests. For these individuals, life is fulfilled by these more basic practices. In those fortunate enough to have time and inclination for esthetic interests, their lives are enhanced further, although the specific esthetic components are individualized.

One's life is best viewed as a process. Judging whether one is leading a Good Life requires looking at the entire process. One's life might differ depending upon various circumstances at different stages. The five major categories outlined in this essay have variable significance among individuals, during life's stages, and because of other existential contingencies. It is the hope of this essay that each of us can understand that he can pursue these ideals in spite of these inequalities or disparities. Each of us has an opportunity to lead the Good Life, as we are responsible for our choices.

Essay 10. Lies, Lying, Liar

Especially, during the pre-election political season, candidates' lies may be raised. It is fitting to explore the meaning or meanings of lies. The definition of a lie is a false statement or falsehood, deliberately presented as being true (41). The agent who is lying is a liar. The etymology of the verb, to lie, is complex, and is confused by the other meanings of lie, related to placement. For example, the book lies on the table, or he wants to lie down. The latter usage is further complicated by having 9 different verb meanings, 3 different noun meanings, and 2 different idiomatic usages (41). All are derived from Old Germanic and Old English; those related to placement have additional Dutch, Norse, Greek, and Latin stems (41).

The precise meaning of words is critical to understanding. For example, someone who lies with another woman is a lie-er (or lyer?) with her, but also a liar to his spouse, as he is breaking his marital vows. Even simple words involving the verb, to be, might be confused, such as the famous, and technically correct, statement that the understanding of an answer to a question might hinge upon the meaning of "is" (42). Further, judging the morality of an action, such as a lie, is often nuanced and depends upon the context and mindset of the actor. The evaluation of lies is a moral issue. This essay explores lies of the first usage above to assist in adjudicating their morality.

Examples of lies elucidate the issues. The popular movie and play, *A Man for All Seasons*, depicts a lurid lie that results in the execution of a noble man for treason. Sir Thomas More was the Lord Chancellor of England during the reign of Henry VIII. Upon the instigation of the King, the Parliament declares Henry the Supreme Head of the Church.

Thomas resigns his position rather than fulfill the demand that all bishops and members of Parliament renounce their allegiance to the Pope. This renunciation provides a pathway for Henry's divorcing his wife and marrying Anne Boleyn.

Later, Thomas refuses to attend Henry and Anne's wedding or to take an oath declaring that the reigning monarch is the Supreme Head of the Church. Thomas never articulates his reasons for these inactions, but the audience knows that he is opposed to the marriage and oath on religious grounds. He is then imprisoned in the Tower of London. He remains scrupulous in failing to verbalize his reasons publicly, as otherwise, he would be committing treason against the King.

Eventually, Thomas is brought to trial and is convicted of treason based upon perjured testimony by Richard Rich, an ambitious man who declares that Thomas indicated to him that the King could not be the Head of the Church. Thereafter, Thomas is executed for treason. Rich is rewarded with an appointment to be Attorney General of Wales.

There are several types of lies or potential lies displayed in this narrative. First, there is Rich's lie, which is obviously telling a falsehood, known to be false by Rich and Thomas (and the audience), and harmful to Thomas, resulting in his death. Rich also benefits from the lie, receiving his quid pro quo appointment. Most would agree that his lie is immoral, an egregious falsehood, that he knows is false, harming another and benefitting himself.

However, one could argue that Rich's lie might have some salutary effects. It allows Henry to remarry and have additional children in the quest for a male heir. A male heir might prevent political disruption similar to the War of the Roses, which preceded the Tudors. Is it morally justified to argue that the ends justify the means, regardless of the depravity of the means?

Do the ends ever justify the means? In Sir Thomas's situation, he could give his oath of support for the King being Head of the Church, his divorce and his marriage to Anne Boleyn. Unless he chooses to share his true beliefs with friends and family, only he and his God would know what was in his heart. It would save his life, his reputation, and the well-being of his family. Clearly, it would be a lie, repudiating his private conscience and his oath to the church, benefitting himself, although not obviously harming Henry. One could argue that his action is morally justified. After all, the remaining bishops and members of Parliament sign on, presumably justified by beneficial future ends.

On the other side of the coin, there are times when bold action is necessary to undercut tyrannical authority. The lies committed in signing the oath to Henry make a mockery of any democratic authority and the word of law. These ends might foster tyranny. The only law is that enunciated by the king, assailing the Magna Carta and Parliament. If no one speaks out about the abridgment of liberty and individual conscience, there is no one left to speak out.

In addition, taking an oath that one doesn't believe is not oath-taking. Making a promise while crossing your fingers in your back is not making a promise. When an oath is broken, it also breaks the concept of an oath. The wayward husband who lies with another woman breaks his marital oath and is a liar to his wife and community.

Further, breaking one's word is held in counterposition to a virtuous life. A liar cannot be trusted. He does not have the courage of his convictions. Owning up to one's actions is a component of responsibility. He cannot be proud of his behavior, which erodes his self-esteem. Breaking an oath or promise may also relate to perceived disloyalty to those closest to him. In summary, a liar who breaks an oath is untrustworthy, cowardly, irresponsible, and disloyal, lacking in self-esteem. It is a wonder that we humans so often take part in these deceptions.

As suggested above, we might go easy on Sir Thomas if he elects to sign the oath, as it does promote some good. Certainly, all of his family and friends would agree to his action. A coerced oath or oath-breaking does not carry the weight of an oath taken more freely, so Thomas's action would have been perceived in that way. Yet, the greatest freedom is displayed when one refuses to take part in activity tyrannically imposed. Those who valiantly disdain acceptance of dictatorial edicts and suffer severe punishment and death show the pinnacle of freedom. We humans know this, which explains the contortions Henry undergoes to convince Thomas to sign the oath. Thomas's refusal has much more of a lasting influence than Henry's tyranny. All dictatorial regimes eventually fall; Thomas's statement lives on.

A better example of a "justifiable lie" occurred when brave Germans protected Jews in their attic as they lied to Nazi officials. Most would agree that the ends (saving some Jews' lives) justified the means (lying), but the Nazi regime did not. In Sir Thomas's case, Henry would agree that the ends (his divorce and remarriage) justifies the means (lying oaths taken by Parliament and Nobles), but the morality is more nuanced. One measure of the morality is the degree to which the lie helps the liar and harms the one to which the lie is directed. The courageous Germans' lies exposed themselves to considerable risk and harm, although the lie also harmed the Nazis, from the Nazis' point of view.

Lies with faulty or incomplete knowledge are not lies in the usual sense, as they are not known to be false. Expressing beliefs, biases, or prejudices are simply stating things that are believed to be true. Extreme examples of these views are enhanced or induced by propaganda. One has little responsibility for these beliefs. However, in a more general sense, one is responsible for trying to be informed of the facts, open to considering alternate viewpoints.

A lighthearted lie might be an "April Fools" duplicity or a canard expressed as a joke. These are not malicious, as they do not benefit the instigator or harm the recipient of the joke. However, there are marginal issues, such as promulgating beliefs in Santa Clause, that might be in opposition to another's religious beliefs.

Other examples of justifiable lies might include the shading or hiding of truth in an effort to protect another from the discomfort of truth. A doctor discussing the prognosis of an elderly husband's illness to his wife might shade the truth in an effort to give hope for recovery. Withholding your thoughts from others is not immoral, as they are your thoughts.

Likewise, the mindset is important in judging other's actions, including those involving untruths. Iago was considered an honorable, honest man by Othello. His contemptible lie, along with Othello's penchant for jealousy, fomented the tragic Othellian downfall and the murder of his faithful wife, Desdemona. It is unclear what benefit Iago might have derived from his lie other that the promotion of evil, as he was the embodiment of Satan himself.

The mindset is also involved when someone owns up to his lies or other improprieties. It should include a heartfelt apology, but often the apologist is merely giving an excuse or justification of his action.

CONCLUSION

When analyzing a lie and its aftermath it is useful to understand the benefit to the liar and the harm to the recipient. Practical jokes involving untruths are not lies in the usual sense and generally do no harm or benefit. Hiding or shading the truth from someone else may at times be the most judicious and moral action one can make, as in the doctor-patient example. The most egregious lies include those of Rich and Iago. Oath-breaking is a special category of lying, harming the offender as much as the offended. Most would agree that the brave Germans' lies to protect some Jews were ethically sound as they clearly fostered good ends while putting the liars at considerable risk. If Thomas lies while taking the oath of allegiance to Henry, he acts immorally while promoting some good, displaying the nuanced nature of adjudicating lying. His refusal to take the oath displays the heights of morality; although, at the time, his wife and family did not share in his belief.

Essay 11. Free Will, Morality, Bias, Prejudice and Racism (43, 44)

Underlying Theme

The underlying theme of this essay is to understand bias, prejudice, and racism, and how these notions are related to our natural free will, responsibility and moral sense. A discussion of freedom, consciousness, responsibility, equality, and morality precede the discussion of bias and racism, in an effort to explain the latter.

Introduction

In the first section, human nature is explored, in an ontological sense, to understand the meaning of freedom, free will, and responsibility. A distinction is made between free will and its accompanying biologic processes, residing in the central nervous system. An individual performing an action, described in common human language, characterizes free will. Individual responsibility is inherent in the action. The parallel neurochemical, physical activity is described by causal language, and is potentially depicted by scientific explanations. A constant duality is seen to be present. Finally, freedom and responsibility are seen to be necessary requirements for moral actions.

The second section deals with the differentiation between moral tenets or beliefs and moral actions. Morality is characterized by a desire to expand equality to those less favored by genetics and acculturation through the voluntary restriction of some liberties from the more fortunate. A moral sense is stressed as being part of our nature. The third section is an expansion of the moral discussion to include biases, prejudice, and racism.

Free Will and the Physical World: the Mind-Body Quandary

The physical world is the world of our senses, described in causal, everyday language and made intelligible by science. The process of experiencing the physical world includes both the sensations and the inferences made about the sensations, which clarify the world. We infer or induce things in explaining them. Causality, time, space and gravity are not experienced directly. Rather they are the fabric of experiences.

The common-sense descriptions of the world are provided by everyday language, consensually reinforced by other people. The words are signs, representing things, and are agreed upon by the use of the same language, a product of our social nature. A third person or a dictionary can often resolve differences of opinions between two humans on things, as the meanings are established by consensus.

The scientific approach to the world uses different procedures. Precise measurements of phenomena and mathematical descriptions are components of the techniques involved. Sophisticated technologies are also used. Often, statistical inferences are made. The usefulness of a theoretical description is measured by the extent to which it provides a deeper understanding of a phenomenon. Further, the theoretical descriptions often allow for predictions of future events. The language of science is couched in the inference that the physical world behaves in a causal manner, similar to the common-sense language.

At an early stage of our development we learn that we can act freely simply by acting. Later we are able to give reasons for our actions in common-sense language. The accompanying physical phenomena are explained in causal language. A simple rendering of this mind-body distinction accepts the obvious duality involved. Inherent in doing an action for a reason are the notions of freedom and responsibility. It is assumed that we could have done otherwise when we perform an action freely. Since we choose to do the action, we have responsibility for it.

It was important to explore our nature, free will, and responsibility, as distinct from the causal physical world, in order to relate these concepts to morality, the subject of the next section.

Morality versus Moral Tenets

A burgeoning discipline is moral psychology, which investigates morality in terms of moral belief systems or tenets. An example of this is provided in the delightfully, readable book by Jonathon Haidt, *The Righteous Mind* (39). The methodology explored utilizes questionnaires of various groups from different cultural backgrounds and other techniques to disclose various beliefs and belief systems embraced by the different groups.

Two broad categories are the secular, Western, progressive group; and the more traditional, religious, conservative group. He quite correctly discloses significant differences between the groups regarding their religious, moralistic, beliefs; and he understands these differences in terms of their cultural and genetic development, their innate nature. Finding six major classes of beliefs – fairness in terms of expressing equality or caring, fairness in terms of treating people equally "under the law," liberty promotion, loyalty to clan or nation, respect for authority, and sanctity – he finds that the secular progressive group favors the first category, fairness in terms of equality and caring, and the latter five categories are more embodied in the beliefs of the traditional group. Further, he shows that these belief systems often control our actions in a reflex-like response.

I should like to explore this configuration in four ways. First, the distinction between these six classes of beliefs will be juxtaposed against the concepts of human virtues. Second, these tenets will be discussed in terms of the two major aspects involved in justice adjudication: equality and liberty. The intrinsic human bases of our free will and liberty, and of our quest to promote equality, will be adduced to explain the primacy of these two aspects of our nature in our political promotion of justice. The importance of the profound differences found within our human species will be presented and related to our desire to promote some equality. Third, the very important distinction between these tenets or canons of our belief systems and our free action as humans will be developed. Fourth, the difference between moral or ethical thinking and these tenets or beliefs will be explored.

Some of these beliefs or canons can be expressed as virtues, each of which has an opposing virtue. An obvious example is pride, which has its opposite, humility; likewise, courage has its opposing virtue, prudence. Loyalty to family, clan, or nation finds its contrary expression in the virtuous courage to counter loyalty for the right reasons (tyranny, for example). Support for property values might oppose virtuous sentiments of charity or taxation to foster some elements of equality. Finally, the virtues expressed in prayerfulness and religious beliefs might find opposition in the virtuous respect for others' beliefs. Virtue is not an all or none affair; similar to morality itself, virtuous behavior is nuanced. There are opposing considerations involved in choosing to do something and in the judgment whether or not the behavior is virtuous.

Two of these value systems, our freedom and our mission to promote some equality, are fundamental aspects of our nature. Similarly, a moral sense is evident. As we cannot use reason to prove the existence of reason, we cannot prove our ability to think morally. But, we could not have a normative discussion without our already believing in our ability to think morally. Otherwise there would be no common basis for discussion. There is a relationship between reasoning and thinking morally, as both are intrinsic components of our nature.

Most political adjudication is mediated between the ideals of liberty and equality. The difficulty in mediating the process is due to the different mindsets of the protagonists favoring the maximizing of liberty and those favoring the advancement of equality. Looking at the six categories of moral tenets or belief systems enunciated by Dr. Haidt, one can see that the tenets embraced by diminishing oppression; loyalty to one's own clan, religion, and belief systems; sanctity, particularly for one's own religious beliefs; respect for the authority of one's clan; support for property rights; and equality in terms of equal protection and adjudication of the law; are enunciated by those favoring liberty. Those favoring equality in terms of caring or fairness express the counterpoised position.

These belief systems or presentiments are not the same as our ability to think morally. The most obvious distinction is evident by these tenets not being invariant. Tyrannical governments can convince people about certain beliefs, as the Nazi indoctrination of the Germans to hate all Jews or the Tutsis to hate all Hutus. Although some of the tendencies are probably genetically determined, parental teaching and clan or group culture can modify them. Further, one can train oneself to behave morally, in the Aristotelian sense, so that one routinely behaves in a certain way. Finally, and most importantly, morality is the process by which we weigh the moral behavior of an action. Even though each individual might have different beliefs one can always act differently. One can look at things from many aspects and adjudicate their value, which is the substance of moral thinking.

For example, someone might have a strong feeling that taxation of the rich is immoral, as it is forcefully removing the prerogative of the individual to deal with his rightful property. But the individual might be persuaded that some taxation to provide for orphans would be reasonable. Another who thinks that everyone's financial income should be identical might be persuaded that this could produce a disincentive for work and thus less productivity and income for everyone. The moral thinking is the innately moral process, not the moral beliefs themselves.

Moral psychologists have made significant contributions in exploring the moral beliefs, tenets, or canons in individuals and different cultural groups. Many of these are outgrowths of our natural requirement to protect our family, our clan, and ourselves from "others." They are often given as reasons for actions. The degree to which the biases influence our behavior reflect upon the degree to which our freedom is lost in the action. Our free will is fundamental to our nature, providing us with a unique characteristic that is not shared by anything else in the universe. Our free will provides for much of the nobility of our species, and for much of its ignominy.

Prejudice, Racism, and Morality

In the first two sections, freedom, a moral sense for some equality, responsibility, and morality are discussed. This section discusses bias, prejudice, and racism in terms of these concepts.

Prejudice and racism are pejorative terms. The definition of prejudice is a set belief based upon ignorance. Although the usage of bias and prejudice has merged throughout the years, the original definition of prejudice being based on ignorance is useful, giving it special meaning beyond bias. A bias is a set belief or predisposition, but does not necessarily imply ignorance. Racism is the acting out of these beliefs on other people, the objects of the beliefs, with the intent to do harm by demeaning them. Racism does not have to be directed at race alone, as its use has been expanded to include gender (for example the female sex, "sexism"), sexual orientation, religion, etc., and its general usage will be maintained here. Racism is also an immoral action.

For example, a Caucasian might make a deprecatory comment to a black African or African-American about his skin color. He might say that his Caucasian race is superior in intelligence, which is clearly not true, is prejudicial, based upon ignorance, and expresses racism. He might also say that African-Americans are innately better basketball players than Caucasians, which may or may not be true, and is neither clearly prejudicial nor racist.

For the purposes of this essay, I should like to keep these definitions of bias, prejudice, and racism as they express three distinct categories. Bias is considered a belief, tenet, or persuasion favoring one group or entity over another, generally determined by genetics or acculturation. Prejudice is a bias based upon ignorance of a known or known facts. Potentially, the prejudice can be ameliorated or eliminated through education.

Racism is a hostile exercise to produce harm on a group or entity based upon bias or prejudice. All three of these categories can be directed against another's race, physical appearance, gender, sexual orientation, nationality, skin color, etc. Again, racism will be used generically for all of these actions.

Beliefs or biases may be fostered by intense cultural activity, or by propaganda, that may be prejudicial. The Nazi regime in Germany prior to and during World War II is a good example of this. The negative characterization of Jews was clearly prejudicial and resulted in the immoral racism practiced against the Jews.

There are many other presentiments, beliefs, and canons that humans have that are a reflection of genetics and acculturation. These beliefs can be fostered by the immersion in one's culture and the teaching and examples of parents, teachers, members of family and clan, and other authority figures. Some of the views are natural outgrowths of our survival needs, as we have to provide for food, shelter, water, and clothing for our family, clan and selves. This requires our being engaged in various activities, broadly included in the designation, work. Conflicts can occur between groups or individuals over limited resources. We exercise our freedom in fulfilling these and our other needs, which is a natural process.

In understanding others and ourselves, it is important to realize that each of us has a set of these tenets or presentiments. Having these beliefs is part of our nature. They are more prominent in some, for genetic or cultural reasons, and, consequently, influence actions in them to a greater degree. Each of us carries biases that are components of or, often, reasons for our free action.

We are a species with wide differences among us, including our physical appearance, body habitus, intelligence, family structure, sexuality, gender, and beliefs. It is natural for these biases and characteristics to influence our actions toward others. This behavior is not unconscionable in itself. Rather, an action needs to be adjudicated and analyzed thoughtfully, using our moral sense.

In some respects, these predispositions are not our responsibility, as we did not effect them. They are a natural outgrowth of our biologic requirement for survival and satisfaction of our basic and secondary needs, and of the cultural milieu in which each of us lives. Our responsibility in these matters is in how we act. The more our actions are reflexive, the less they show our freedom and responsibility. Our responsibility is entailed when we thoughtfully explain our actions in terms of the biases. The most unconscionable action is one that is based on one of these predisposing values, even when we know, morally, that the action is wrong. The most ennobling action is one that opposes some of these inherent tendencies through analysis of the morality of the action.

For example, someone might join a book club so that he can interact with others of similar interests. Another might belong to a charitable organization as he feels that equality should be fostered. Most of these presentiments are not obviously true or false, so are not necessarily prejudicial. They are not immoral in themselves, but can be the object of moral thinking. The bibliophile might indicate that everyone should read at least two hours daily, which is a reflection of his belief in education. The central government should enforce this by necessitating a two-hour time block for reading for any employment. As this plays out in the political arena, it is obvious that this would unduly restrict the liberty of employers. Although not clearly prejudicial, it would be harmful to the non-bibliophiles, thus racist. The bias toward reading is not immoral in itself. But this execution of the bias would be immoral and racist.

Many individual predispositions are not always prejudicial, in the sense of being founded on ignorance, and are potentially malleable. One might have an underlying belief that expansion of liberty and freedom is preferred fundamentally over the expansion of equality. The morality of the position is evident in its modulation between these two aspects of our nature, both individually and politically.

Further examples make these points more clearly. Does the fact that 96% of African-Americans voted for Barack Obama mean that African-Americans are expressing prejudice? Or, Americans of Irish ancestry voting overwhelmingly for John F. Kennedy? I suspect both were mostly natural expressions of support for their own bias rather than prejudice. No teaching would alter the fact that they are who they are, and they and the presidential candidate share some mutual identity.

Nor do they express racism. Supporting kin and clan is a natural outgrowth of our liberty and freedom, exercised to protect our clan and us. These actions are not racist or immoral unless there is the direct intent to do harm. Some of these biases can be tempered through cultural immersion and familiarity of different people, although, sometimes, the immersion or confrontations reinforce the biases.

Racism need not be directed at another's race per se. It can be directed at some other characteristic. An obese person can be called "fatso," or a "pig." A person of short stature might receive the epithets, "shorty" or "shrimp boat." In each case, there is an intention to compartmentalize the person in a demeaning manner. People are insulted when they are considered by one characteristic alone, especially when expressed in a deprecating manner.

Although a racial slur by a Caucasian to an African-American would be racist, the same term might not be racist if used by an African-American. The importance of intent to do harm or to insult is necessary for the racist label to be used.

Religious beliefs provide other examples of bias that are not obviously prejudicial. No amount of teaching can definitely settle the question of the existence of God. Further, the truth of some of the teachings of religion cannot be settled intellectually, although there can be some modifications of the beliefs through acculturation and teaching. Some of the food proscriptions of some religions have been modified with education. For example, the Roman Catholic faith has modified its fish on Fridays rule.

Religious beliefs also become reasons for actions. It is in these actions that morality is tested. Roman Catholic voters favored John F. Kennedy by a large margin. This is not immoral in itself, but it can be modified, especially if potential reasons for doing otherwise are convincing. Your good Protestant friend could convince you that there might be repression of freedom of Protestants with a Roman Catholic president, or he might indicate that a Roman Catholic president would do the bidding of the Pope rather than represent the entire populace. (Even though these fears never materialized, they still could have been reasonable subjects for consideration). The morality of the action is not immediately evident, but requires judgment, whether or not there is intent to do harm to a group, based upon a biased belief.

There are other situations when the morality involving religious beliefs is more serious and provide justification for mortal conflicts with others. Christians during the Crusades, holy Islamic wars against non-believers, and the killing of Protestants by Roman Catholics in Northern Ireland and vice versa are obvious examples. These demonstrate religious expansionism coming into direct conflict with other basic, religious tenets. Our moral sense argues for equality among humans. The commandment not to kill and the virtues of forgiveness, charity, and humility are in contradistinction to war and hostile behavior.

Similarly, the religious belief in the sanctity of heterosexual marriage is conflicted with the belief in egalitarianism in the approach to same-sex couples. The morality is nuanced and plays out both individually and politically. The basic religious belief in God is not challenged in this intercourse, nor is it prejudicial. But some of the teachings as bases for actions may be reasons promoting racism and immorality. Seen from the other side, legal encroachment on religious beliefs about the sanctity of heterosexual marriage might be viewed as racism against the religion and its practitioners.

Prejudice, bias, racism, and morality are more complex with beliefs that are not acted on others. Further, another might not know the reasons for an action, as the reasons are not public unless someone chooses to give his reasons. Even then, is it immoral or racist for someone to have a prejudicial bias against another race, so long as it is not acted out on the human stage? Is it obviously immoral for someone to share these beliefs with his trusted family? One is not generally responsible for his beliefs or biases, which may have been largely out of his control (genetically or culturally developed).

In conclusion, biases and prejudices are natural expressions of our nature, resulting from our need to protect ourselves from "the others," especially when resources are limited. We are not clearly responsible for most of these beliefs, as they are largely the result of genetics and one's culture. The beliefs are not immoral themselves; racism and immorality occur when they come into play in human interaction. They can be modified by our moral sense and reason. We are mostly ennobled when we examine our underlying presentiments, and then act accordingly, when judged morally appropriate.

How should we deal with ourselves in the light of this discussion? First, self-examination allows us to see our own biases. Part of this examination would include separating out prejudices from biases, when additional knowledge would be illuminating. Most of our biases are harmless and should be perceived in that light. Rooting for a college football team should not be considered immoral or racist. Likewise, voting for someone of your ethnic background is natural and not overtly harmful to others. Biases per se are not immoral or racist. However, judging the morality of how biases play out in human actions is sometimes difficult and should be based upon whether actions are done to promote harm to others or not.

SECTION IV. HUMAN NATURE AND POLITICAL ACTION

This section of political action expands the discussions of human nature and morality, and the dynamic between liberty and equality. Essay 12 examines population control and abortion; Essay 13 discusses governmental regulatory involvement in global warming. Essay 15 involves heterosexual and homosexual unions. Essays 14 and 16 include governmental involvement in health care and in nutrition, respectively. It is apparent in these five essays that the political expansion of equality is favored by those with progressive or liberal points of view; the retention of liberties by the conservative.

Essay 12. Population Control, Birth Control, and Abortion Rights (45)

Some of the problems ensuing from the rapid expansion of the human population are starvation and malnutrition from limited food supplies and water in many population centers, possible global warming and its consequences from human activity, and further disparities between the "haves" and the "have-nots." Whereas technological advances might ameliorate some of these eventualities, most would agree that there are overall benefits for control of the world's population.

Issues regarding population are different for each nation. A decreasing population in well-developed countries has a negative impact on economic expansion and world influence, which can influence immigration policies. Positions on birth control and immigration are necessary for each nation and the world at large.

Various considerations impact on the legality and methods employed for birth control. This is an obvious example of the political interactions between liberty and equality. Fostering birth control by various methods expands equality affording more resources for all. However, this may come at the price of restricting some liberties, including those of individuals, states, religious entities, and the unborn fetus.

Methods of Birth Control

There are at least nine categories of population control: (1) encouragement of chastity and avoidance of premarital sexual activity; (2)

avoidance of sexual activity during ovulation ("rhythm"); (3) use of condoms or diaphragms; (4) anovulatory medications (birth control pills); (5) medication to prevent embryo implantation in the uterus (the "morning after" pill); (6) elective surgical sterilization (vasectomy, tubal ligation, or hysterectomy); (7) termination of pregnancy (early pregnancy or late-term pregnancy) by chemical or surgical means; (8) political programs to decrease the population (number of children allowed per couple, destruction of groups considered unfavorable, eugenically determined population control; and (9) infanticide. Clearly, there are gradations in terms of moral or religious objections, with the earlier categories being the least objectionable and state control and infanticide being the most.

Restriction of the free expression of chastity or the practice of the rhythm method for birth control would be inappropriate infringements of liberty. On the other hand, these should not be foisted upon everyone, as that would be tyrannical imposition. Likewise, abolition of the voluntary use of birth control pills, condoms and diaphragms are unconscionable limitations of liberty. Also, governmental advocacy of these practices would be an overreach (for example, supplying condoms in public schools or insisting that Roman Catholics pay taxes for birth control). Religious and moral freedoms must be supported in democratic societies.

Rights of the Infant, Intra-uterine Fetus, Embryo before Implantation, Sperm and Ova

The major problems with the political institution of population control occur with considerations of the last four categories. A discussion of the rights and special dignity of the infant, the intra-uterine fetus, the embryo before uterine implantation, and the sperm and ova is necessary to clarify the moral issues involved. The sperm and ova have biologic significance, but each sperm and ovum does not have special significance. Sperm are produced and lost continuously until senescence, and the female complement of ova are gradually lost during one's lifetime. Each gamete, however, has the full chromosomal expression of the somatic parent cells, the sperm providing either an X or Y chromosome, and the ovum only an X chromosome.

The fertilized ovum, the human embryo, on the other hand, contains the potential for the development of a unique human, expressing the genetic characteristics of both parents. However, the embryo is incapable of developing into a human on its own, as it requires implantation in and evolution within the human uterus. Presumably, many embryos are formed, but only one or a few undergo implantation in the uterus, most being lost through natural biologic processes. All of the potentialities for the eventual birth of a unique human are contained within the implanted human embryo.

Although some implanted embryos are naturally lost (miscarriage or natural abortion), each has this special feature. The gradual development of the embryo or fetus and delivery as an infant is a continuous process. Although there may be a time when the fetus is potentially capable of sustaining life outside of the uterus (20 or 24 weeks), it is difficult to predict.

Most agree that the sperm and ovum do not have special rights, except that they belong to the parent, unless these rights are given away legally for artificial insemination or ovum donation. The fertilized ovum and the developing embryo, however, possess a nobility of their own, and require special consideration, as they are potentially unique humans, requiring implantation in a uterus or an in vitro process. Once implantation occurs, another milestone is reached. With each developmental stage, the fetus becomes more human in utero, and the maturing baby ex utero continues this maturing process. Babies and children require diligent care and education to foster this development.

The rights of the new human increase along this continuum, making it difficult to state when these rights should be exerted outside their parents. Regardless, it can be argued that the embryo/fetus/child has special dignity at each stage. Religious institutions do not have to resort to vague concepts such as time of ensoulment of the fetus. Rather, it can be argued on a secular level that the developing human has special dignity, which increases incrementally with development.

Guidelines for Political Action

The most reasonable guidelines for legislative action should attempt to make abortion safe for the mother (fostering equality) and free for the mother to decide whether to have the abortion (which is the law of the land and should remain legal, which fosters her liberty), but should be rare (promoting freedom and some equality for the unborn child). Methods of birth control earlier in the continuous development from germ cell to living child should be promulgated. Regardless of any de jure designation, de facto, the mother has a right to this choice.

Both "pro-choice" and "pro-life" advocates should support the safety of the procedure, which include assurances that places for abortion are sanitary and meet accepted medical and surgical standards of care. Legal requirements for procedures that are not medically required, such as vaginal or transabdominal ultrasound examinations should not be a required component of the monitoring process, as their enforcement unnecessarily infringes upon the mother's liberty. Counseling ought to be available, but not required, as the procedure might be psychologically damaging. Preferably, the option for adoption should be discussed as part of the counseling process. All should agree that abortion should not be the preferred method of birth control, and that methods for contraception should be discussed to prevent further unwanted pregnancies.

In the same sense that "pro-life" advocates should be respectful of the legal right of the mother to choose, "pro-choice" proponents should respect the moral and religious beliefs and sentiments of those opposed to abortion. For example, public funds should not be used to support contraceptive or abortion practices. If public funds are considered, they should be obtained through private charitable institutions. Finally, special moral and religious considerations are required when pregnancy ensues from rape or when the health of the mother is in jeopardy.

The most objectionable practices of population control are those that completely ignore the rights of the unborn or recently born child, including infanticide. Termination of pregnancy for eugenic considerations, such as limiting the number of female children in China, is morally repugnant and ought to be eschewed.

CONCLUSION

Considerations of population control involve moral and political issues. The freedom of the parents and unborn child are juxtaposed and are measured by our moral sense and play out in the political arena. They also involve our esthetic and religious notions, in our expressions of our human dignity.

Essay 13. Governmental Involvement in Planetary Warming

Introduction

Fossil fuels are a limited resource and the development of alternate sources of energy, preferably sustainable and renewable, will be necessary in the long run. Measures to consume fossil fuels economically, with diminished waste discharged into the atmosphere, is consistent with our need to protect our environment. Advocates of both progressive and conservative political philosophies have embraced conservation and preservation of the air, water, and environment of our beautiful planet.

The United States' Environmental Protective Agency (EPA) has been responsible for significant improvements in the quality of our air and water, which should be applauded by those of all political persuasions. These have come at some price, restricting liberty with regulations and rules for industrial waste and some taxation. This expansion of equality, providing an improved planet for all of us, was clearly worthwhile. Restricting our freedom further by expanding environmental policies and rules to diminish human contribution to global warming is hotly debated and is the subject of this essay.

Both sides of the debate agree that we are in a warming climate interlude since the last glaciation ended about 12,000 years ago. The two contrasting scientific views are on the rapidity of the rise in the Earth's temperature and the effect of human activity on planetary warming.

The difficulties with climate research and predictions are obvious when they are compared to weather. Although weather prognostication has improved, it is difficult for meteorologists accurately to predict on a local level beyond one week. Climate change involves the entire Earth and deals with changes over decades, centuries, and millennia.

The two primary issues are quantifying the global rise in temperatures, and assessing the effect of human activity on the rise. There are also subsidiary issues. The first is the history of the various ice ages and glaciations, and the intervening warmer phases, obtained from geologic studies during Earth's 4.6 billion years. This long-term history needs to be related to the current warming phase. Data on climatology measurements during the current interglacial, and, especially, over the past three centuries are important for this issue.

Physicochemical phenomena, potentially resulting in detrimental or salutary effects on our planet, need to be explored. These include the effects of glaciers melting during warm phases and ice accumulation during glaciations; the effect of increased CO_2 on plant growth; the salutary effect of increased atmospheric CO_2 on green plant water requirements and increased oxygen production; the $CaCO_3$ cycle, its role in acidifying the seas, its effect on plant (plankton) growth, and negative and positive feedback mechanisms engaged in its effects; the expansion of the oceans during the warmest phases; and the effects of glaciations on plant and animal life.

A discussion of the effects of humans is required. These include fossil fuel combustion; deforestation; and increased particulate matter and other potentially harmful substances emitted into our atmosphere, including "greenhouse gases" and gases that disrupt the atmospheric ozone layer.

All of this information should be related to models predicting the climate over the next two centuries. Finally, the most rational approaches to influence these processes should be proposed, balanced against their effects on individual nations' economies.

Geologic History, Ice Ages, and Glaciations

We have been in a warming phase since the relaxation of the last glaciation, 12,000 years ago. The most dramatic evidence was the closure of the land bridges between Alaska and Asia, and between Africa and Eurasia to Australia. There have also been minor climatic variations within the current warm interlude, especially the "mini-ice age," Maunder Minimum, from about 1645-1715 CE, presumably due to a halt in sun spot activity and less solar, radiant energy. To put our current interglacial, Holocene Epoch, into perspective, it is instructive to look at Earth's cooling and warming history during its 4.6 Billion years.

Geologists have divided Earth's time intervals according to the developments of life (22). The Hadean Eon was lifeless, lasting about 600 million years, until four billion years before the current epoch (BYBCE). Prokaryotic life, identified and dated by analyzing fossil remains, ushered in the Archean Eon, which lasted until 2.5 BYBCE. Green plants and photosynthesis produced oxygenation of the atmosphere during this eon and mono-cellular animal life developed. The Proterozoic Eon ensued thereafter, lasted 1.9 billion years, and was characterized by multicellular organisms. Thence, large life forms appeared in the Phanerozoic Eon, which began 600 million years before the current epoch (MYBCE), and is ongoing.

The Phanerozoic Eon is divided into the Paleozoic, Mesozoic, and Cenozoic Eras. The Paleozoic lasted until 250 million years ago, during which large, terrestrial plants and animals, including mammals, appeared. The Mesozoic, lasting until 65 million years ago, was considered the age of the dinosaurs, and ended with their mass extinction and the dominance of mammals in the Cenozoic, which is ongoing.

The Cenozoic Era is divided into the Tertiary Period, during which primates appeared, and the Quaternary, when hominids are first seen in 8 MYBCE. The Quaternary has the Pleistocene Epoch, ending with the closure of the land bridges from the last glaciation, into the Holocene Epoch, 12,000 years ago.

Cold spells during this long history are designated as ice ages, which last millions of years, and shorter, glaciations, which last centuries. Two ice ages occurred in the Archean Eon, 2.9 and 2.2 BYBCE, but none other until the Proterozoic Eon. Perhaps the most brutal ice age, in terms of its effect on life, occurred from 750 to 580 million years ago. Three major glaciations ensued during this interval, with total, or nearly total, ice coverage of the entire planet. Life was restricted to the unfrozen depths of the oceans.

Characterizing and dating these events are much more difficult during the older events due to a relative paucity of fossils and other material. The data are more reliable from the Paleozoic Era, during which two ice ages are identified, in the Devonian and Permian Periods, around 400 and 300 MYBCE, respectively. Thereafter, there were no ice ages until 2.5 MYBCE in the Pleistocene and the current Holocene Epochs.

Data are more complete for this current ice age, deriving temperatures by radioisotope techniques from ice cores obtained from the Antarctic (46). As many as 18 glaciations and intervening warm spells have been described. The glaciations have lasted in the range of 200,000 years and the interglacials for much shorter intervals, 10,000-30,000 years.

Within this geologic history, hominids began their existence in a relatively warm period, 8 million years ago, before the current ice age began 2.5 million years ago. Thereafter, humans have survived 18 prolonged glaciations with relatively brief interglacial warming spells. We are currently within an interglacial, perhaps midway, before the next glaciation begins.

Global Warming, Historical

Glaciations have major effects on the oceans, as the glaciers draw up their water, lowering sea levels by as much as 400 feet, changing the contours of continents. The process occurs in reverse with global warming. Temperature data documenting warming are difficult to obtain, particularly prior to the current Phanerozoic Eon, starting 600 million years ago. Indirect measurements of fossils with analysis of their oxygen radioisotopes are required. When the lighter O-16 (oxygen-16), contained in the melting water of glaciers, drains into the sea, the oceans become "lighter" in oxygen, signifying warming. The oxygen data from fossils from various times allow for estimates of temperatures. Other radioisotope techniques are employed to date the fossils.

Also, warming was influenced by the gradual increase in the energy emitted by the sun, as it consumed its hydrogen in nuclear fusion, producing helium. Astronomical observations of similarly-sized stars suggest that the sun might have been as little as 25% as bright during the Hadean Eon as in our current Holocene Epoch. This warming is partially balanced by the cooling of Earth's molten magma.

In addition, a protective ozone layer was absent prior to green plants and photosynthesis. This allowed for increased penetration through the oxygen deprived atmosphere. There were very high concentrations of methane and carbon dioxide, functioning as "greenhouse gases," due to volcanic activity. On balance, Earth's temperature had to be above freezing, at least in the depths of the oceans, to allow the development of life when it began during the Archean Eon.

Astronomical variations also influence the degree of warming, including variations in Earth's orbit around the sun; the influence of the moon, which is gradually spinning away; and precession or oscillations of Earth's orbit (46). These three astronomical changes have been used to predict the occurrence of glaciations and interglacial warming during our current ice age (46). The interglacial warming spells, as determined by radioisotope techniques, have occurred at about 200,000 year intervals, which were predicted by these mathematical formulations. Estimates of how widely average global temperatures have varied, but some have suggested that the Earth has been considerably warmer during other times in the past two million years than in our current epoch. We are probably close to midpoint in the current interglacial, which began 12,000 years ago. The last glacial maximum was estimated to be 20,000-25,000 years ago (46). It is uncertain when the current phase will revert to a cooling one, toward another glaciation.

Warming was particularly intense during episodes of mass extinctions. The more severe occurred in the Mesozoic Era, caused by cataclysmic volcanic eruptions (47). The most massive was at the junction of the Permian and Triassic Periods. Perhaps 90% of life was extinguished. Four other mass extinctions occurred during the Mesozoic, when there was one large continent, Pangea, and one ocean. Brutal volcanos released gas and particulate matter into the atmosphere. Halide gases destroyed the ozone layer. Greenhouse gases, especially carbon dioxide and methane, blocked Earth's radiation and promoted global warming. Estimates of atmospheric CO_2 levels from that time of 3000 ppm have been made (46, 47). Another massive extinction ensued 65 MYBCE, with the extinction of dinosaurs. This was probably related to a huge meteorite landing in the Gulf of Mexico, but may have been accompanied by volcanism.

Although volcanism and extinctions have occurred throughout the Cenozoic Era, none has been as severe as those occurring on Pangea during the Mesozoic (47). This has been related to the breaking-up of the supercontinent. Tectonic plate movements shifting land masses have been well documented geologically, fundamentally related to convection of the Earth's contents. This up and down motion induces drifting of land masses. The development of Pangea and its breaking up, which is continuing, was due to these tectonic movements (47).

Volcanism, confirmed by the presence of large igneous provinces, co-incided temporally with fossil studies showing massive extinctions. At least 5 massive extinctions occurred during the time of Pangea. In spite of episodes of severe volcanism during the past 160 million years, there have been fewer extinctions in the fossil record. The breakup of Pangea might have had a salutary effect on global warming (47).

The severity of the extinctions that occurred in the Mesozoic was prob-ably related to Pangea's size. Warming produces more evaporation of water from the oceans and increased rainfall. However, Pangea's large expanses of interior land, distant from the ocean, received little rain. Rain induces increased weathering of surface and crust limestone by leaching bicarbonates and carbonates, delivering them into the ocean. This draws carbon dioxide chemically from the atmosphere.

Further, the continent's large surface area contained less shoreline, hence less algae formation. There were less algae to convert carbon di-oxide into organic compounds on the Pangea continent. In smaller con-tinents, increased rain also drains more nutrients and chemicals into the ocean, promoting more plant life, augmenting photosynthetic activity.

Most agree that there has been a warming trend over the past 300 years, and some estimates have suggested that each decade has been warmer than the preceding one for the past 150 years. Of course the difficulty with these estimates is the reliability of average global temperature estimates during earlier decades. Measurements for the past 25 years are more reliable, but there has been less of a measurable increase in the global temperature than previously predicted.

There remain uncertainties over the best methods for measuring glob-al temperature, including ocean versus land, frequency and number of locations, and atmospheric versus terrestrial. Further, it is unclear whether it is more relevant to track the highest, lowest, or average temperatures of the day; or whether terrestrial, oceanic, tropospheric, or deeper atmospheric temperatures are more appropriate. Regardless, most of the curves of the various measurements run in parallel.

Physicochemical Changes with Warming, Greenhouse Effect, Ocean pH

Physicochemical changes coincident with the current warming trend have been observed. There is evidence of a rise in the ocean levels, perhaps related to glacier melting. The reliability of these measurements is open to some question, but the rise is expected as the oceans have risen during previous interglacial periods. Predictions on the rapidity and extent of the rise are less certain. Even data on the melting of glaciers have been debated. Although rapid melting of the arctic glaciers is apparent, a similar trend has not been observed in the Antarctic. Antarctic glaciers comprise 90% of the Earth's ice, whereas Greenland contains only 4% (46).

The documentation of the rise of atmospheric CO2 is much more solid. Since increased levels of small gaseous molecules, such as CO2, can trap heat in the atmosphere, global warming might ensue, the so-called greenhouse effect. Methane is another, potent greenhouse gas, produced by animal fermentation, in the digestion of plants. It is also released by volcanism and disruption of the Earth's crust, which contains methane. In addition, there are considerable losses of methane to the atmosphere with drilling for oil and hydraulic fracturing.

The greenhouse effect is due to the absorption by the atmosphere of terrestrially emitted, infrared radiant energy and then re-radiated back to the Earth's surface. The absorption of this energy is augmented by the presence of atmospheric greenhouse gases. Increasing atmospheric CO2, then, should promote global warming. Some have argued that the current rise in global temperature is largely due to the rise in atmospheric CO2, mostly from human activity.

The problem with this thesis is the observation that the rise in CO_2 has been much faster than the rise in measured temperatures. Rising atmospheric, oceanic, and terrestrial temperatures should be apparent from the effect of increased greenhouse gases. There is little controversy whether humans have been responsible for most of the recent rise in atmospheric CO_2. The issues involve ascribing relative responsibility to fossil fuel consumption, to other human activities, such as deforestation, or to natural effects, such as forest fires, and in adjudicating the relative harmful and beneficial effects of atmospheric CO_2.

One salutary effect of elevated atmospheric CO_2 levels is the encouragement of plant growth, which is dependent upon CO_2 for photosynthesis, and functions as a feedback system to decrease atmospheric CO_2. Green plant photosynthesis releases O_2, which can encourage animal growth. There are additional data that the stomata of leaves are modified by higher concentrations of CO_2, which decrease the requirement for water consumption by plants (46).

There is a dynamic involving crust and plate carbonates and bicarbonates; atmospheric and ocean CO_2 levels; water, $NaCl$, $NaHCO_3$ (weak base), H_2CO_3 (weak acid); $CaCl_2$, shell carbonates ($CaCO_3$ and bicarbonate); and organic limestone accretion on the ocean floor and in the Earth's crust. As discussed above, there is more weathering in smaller continents than in the supercontinent, Pangea. Smaller continents allow the rain to reach their arid interiors more easily. The effect of increased rainfall on atmospheric CO_2 is elucidated by two chemical reactions.

First, Atmospheric: $CO_2 + H_2O + NaCl = NaHCO_3 + HCl$ (Eq. 1). In words, the atmospheric CO_2 combines with water and salt to produce sodium bicarbonate (bicarbonate of soda, a weak base); and the strong acid, hydrochloric acid (hence its designation, acid rain). The produced $NaHCO_3$, additional $NaHCO_3$ and Na_2CO_3 in the Earth's crust, and HCl are washed into the sea.

Next, Terrestrial and Ocean: 2NaHCO3 + CaCl2 = CaCO3 + 2NaCl + H2O + CO2 (Eq. 2). In words, sodium bicarbonate reacts with calcium chloride (another salt in river waters and oceans), producing limestone (eventually found in the shells of shellfish, and in the ocean's floors), salt, water, and carbon dioxide. Note that two bicarbonates, derived from equation 1 are consumed for each molecule of CO2 produced in equation 2, for a net loss of atmospheric CO2.

Recent information on ocean acidification has suggested a rise (a drop in pH). Plankton growth is pH-dependent. Most of the ocean's food is derived directly or indirectly from these unicellular plants in a superficial ocean layer. However, it should also be noted that CO2 is a weak acid, as it forms H2CO3 (carbonic acid) in water. When CO2 evaporates from the heated ocean, acid is removed from the ocean. In a sense, the acidic CO2 removed from the atmosphere during weathering is balanced by the addition of acid to the atmosphere from evaporation. Levels of atmospheric and oceanic CO2 and carbonic acid have varied considerably during our planet's existence, through which plankton have survived, largely due to these chemical processes.

Weathering also brings more nutrients into the ocean, which fosters plant growth. The augmented photosynthesis removes additional CO2 from the atmosphere. Further, plankton flourish in the shallower waters, preferentially around land masses. The dissolution of the Pangea supercontinent provided more of these regions. Further, some of the plankton that evolved since Pangea's demise are coccoliths, which are able to convert ocean CO2 to shells, further diminishing ocean CO2 and acidity (47).

Warming has positive reinforcing aspects also. The glacier melting allows for less reflection of radiant energy from the sun and more permafrost release of CH4. The increase in forest fires due to warming also releases more CO2 and diminishes plant life and photosynthesis.

Recent Data on Climate Variables, 2014-2016 (48)

Global warming accelerated over the past three years. Global sea surface temperatures reached record highs in 2014, 2015, and 2016. Although this rise was consistent with the warming trend from 1981-2010, the rise was more pronounced in 2014 and 2015.

The apparent accelerated rise may be explained by strong El Niño and weak La Niña events. Typically the eastern Pacific discharges its deep, cold waters to the surface, leaving western North America cool. Every decade or so, El Niño supervenes and represses this rise, yielding warmer conditions. La Niña follows during the next year leaving colder than usual conditions. The El Niño was stronger and the La Niña weaker than usual during the 2015-2016 seasons. Although the events are initiated in the eastern Pacific, the warming and cooling effects occur worldwide.

By four methodologies, sea levels continued to follow the rising trend since 1993 (by 3-8 cms), although there was a slight decrement in 2016, perhaps related to La Niña cooling.

The atmospheric CO_2 continued to rise to 402.9 ppm, which is the highest recorded atmospheric value. By ice core measurements of CO_2, dated by radioisotope techniques, this level is the highest value for the past 600,000 years (48). However, estimates have been made of atmospheric CO_2 during massive extinctions as high as 3000 ppm (47).

The Effects of Humans on the Planet

In addition to increased atmospheric CO_2, other obvious negative effects of humans on our planet include deforestation, uncontrolled mining, exhaustion of natural resources, poor handling of waste (organic, nuclear, mineral, batteries, automobiles, tires, etc.), and poor management of erosion and arable soil (49). The EPA has been effective in decreasing the release of particulate matter and aerosolized halogenated gases into the atmosphere. The latter has helped to restore and preserve the atmospheric ozone layer. In addition, the EPA has been instrumental in improving fresh water quality.

CONCLUSION

Climate science, similar to other sciences, should be open to analysis, should continue to accrue pertinent data, and should not be considered a closed issue. There should not be heated debate over the presence or absence of climate change, which should be answered with quantitative measurements. As discussed above, we are in the midst of an interglacial period characterized by warming since the end of the last glaciation. The critical questions are the degree of change, the influence of humans on climate, and the appropriate policies that should be advocated regarding climate. A reasonable baseline might be 1998, as most would agree that measurements obtained since then are more reliable. Nearly 25 years of very complete data have been compiled. Earlier studies need not be excluded, especially if they reinforce the recently acquired, more complete information. Worldwide terrestrial, ocean, and atmospheric temperatures; atmospheric CO_2 concentrations; oceanic acidity, levels, and plant life, particularly plankton and other monocellular microorganisms; and depth of glaciers are particularly relevant.

It should also be understood that we are midway in our current interglacial warming period. It is not known when average temperatures will begin to fall toward the next glaciation. Our greater threat may eventually be global cooling rather than warming.

Organizations responsible for accumulating and evaluating the information must avoid bias. Contrary opinions should be welcomed and debated. Although the reports from the Intergovernmental Panel on Climate Change are publicized and available for critique, there has been considerable controversy over the published opinions and summaries. Governmental policy should be directed by science and economic conditions.

Since local events occur on relatively small areas of the Earth's surface, it is likely that they are usually not related to global warming. Local heat or cold waves, El Niño and La Niña effects, hurricanes, and tornadoes are much more likely to be due to local weather events. Measured theories about this, however, should be encouraged and opened to the scientific community, based upon scientific studies.

Predictive models should continue to be utilized based on the best information available, with the realization that they are limited. The models should be modified and/or abandoned if they do not describe the data.

Discussions on climate change should be concurrent with other environmental issues, including our outstripping of natural resources, worldwide poverty, waste disposal, mining, deforestation, and political institutions. Whereas capitalism has brought about many salutary changes, when unfettered, it has also promoted environmental damage. Inclusive, rather than extractive, political institutions should be fostered, allowing everyone to have a stake in the game (49, 50). These complex discussions are best considered in terms of the planet as a whole. Many of our human problems are aggravated by overpopulation, a Malthusian effect. Historically, wars, famine, and plagues have limited overpopulation. We should hope that our problems could be settled more rationally.

Research into alternate energy sources should be encouraged. Everyone desires renewable, sustainable energy. Putting humanity's history into perspective is useful. Humans, similar to us, have only been present for the past 100,000-300,000 years, with most of the time spent within the 18 glaciations of the current ice age (23, 24). Humans have survived this ice age through their ingenuity. Our current interglacial, Holocene Epoch, has been extant for only 12,000 years. Civilizations began during this epoch, but written history for only half of it. The industrial revolution was initiated just two and a half centuries ago. Human ingenuity is our most important resource in solving planetary problems, including sustainable energy.

Private enterprise should be encouraged in this development, as the market place favors the most cost-effective approaches. A technological advance in solar batteries is an obvious example. Photosynthesis, capturing the sun's photons in chemical reactions involving carbon dioxide and water, is nearly 100% efficient. The conversion of corn to liquid fuel is an attempt to capitalize on this process, but it may be technically and economically disadvantageous. The photosynthetic reactions involve carbon dioxide, water, enzymatic catalysts, and a somewhat mysterious process of "quantum tunneling" (8, 9). Fundamental understanding and technologic harnessing of this process may ensue in the near future.

Geothermal energy, more complete combustion of coal in electricity generating stations, and improved retrieval of methane (natural gas) with hydraulic fracturing and oil drilling are other examples.

The political and economic realities of each nation have to be evaluated individually. For example, too much restriction of oil and natural gas availability in developing countries might encourage burning of incompletely combusted coal or peat, or deforestation with wood burning.

Dealing with global warming's effects will be necessary, regardless of the amount contributed by human activity. This includes aiding populated coastal areas with dykes, shifts of homes to inland locations, etc. Since there is overlap among many efforts involved in preserving our planet, such as deforestation, population control, war and civil disorder, and clean water, it would be prudent to design programs that assist all.

Finally, it should be recognized that the presence of humans has produced significant changes in the ecology of our Earth. In our quest to preserve animal and plant species, we have to remember that humans are a component of the evolutionary processes that are taking place. There have always been extinctions of some species. This will continue and probably expand as humankind's influence on the Earth increases. Preservation of the natural beauty of our air, water, forests, and other features should be encouraged. Each of us should do his part in conservation, including minimizing fossil fuel use, which has many salutary benefits. The dictum from Genesis is true that we have dominion over the animals, plants, and the Earth; but we are also charged with being responsible caretakers. Addressing climate change in terms of its understanding and possible amelioration of its effects is one of our duties as responsible citizens of our planet.

Essay 14. Governmental Involvement in Health Care (51)

Ideally, laws should promote things for the polis that are good for an individual and for his interaction with other individuals. Those laws should relate to our human nature (52). Although there may be some controversies regarding the genetic and environmental mix in the genesis of our nature, most reasonable people agree to its presence. We learn at an early age that each of us is comprised of a self, of which we are self-conscious. We see that we can act freely, simply by doing things that involve our physical bodies. Avoiding the epistemic question of how a free agent can cause something to happen, the mind-body philosophical problem, one has the belief early in childhood that he is free to do something simply by doing it; he brings it about. A necessary accompaniment of this free action is responsibility for the action.

In addition, it is clear that there are significant inequalities among us, especially regarding aspects that improve our ability to get on through our lives. Physical health is one of the obvious examples. We are a biological species with physiologic needs, including food, water, shelter, and clothing; and some additional needs including preservation of our species, love, sex, and self-esteem. Some aggressive aspects of our nature allow for fulfillment of these needs since there may be competition for limited resources.

We also have a moral sense. It is impossible to have an ethical controversy unless there is a moral basis upon which actions can be judged. Our moral nature is evident in feelings of compassion and altruism, sometimes resulting in charity, which promotes some equality. Conversely, the moral sense is perceived when we experience shame or guilt as we rue our immoral behavior. Finally, we are social beings, reflected in our language, establishing the presence of others. This social aspect of our nature results in attempts to regulate our behavior along lines consistent with our natural moral sense.

This usually plays out between unrestricted liberty, at one extreme, and egalitarianism at the other. A model for the political process is the maintenance of as much liberty as possible, restricting it only for very good reasons in the enhancement of some equality. As egalitarianism is fostered, there is a reciprocal loss of some of our freedom.

Political expression, concepts of justice and fairness, are negotiated between these two facets of our nature. For example, the distribution of goods and services to those who have less can be promoted through taxation of those who have more. There is a necessary tension between these elements until an appropriate balance is reached. Legal institutions, laws, and precedents are established, balancing these aspects of our nature to promote the common good and to maximize liberty and equality.

Turning to the legal framework supporting governmental involvement in health care, we see that there are a number of issues, including the following three: 1. What is the current status of how doctors practice medicine, how is quality of the practice measured, and how is quality promulgated? Should the government be involved in judging quality of medical practice and in the enforcement of perceived good quality? If so, how is the enforcement effected? 2. What is the cost of expanding insurance coverage to those currently uninsured and how is it financed? Are there downsides to the expansion other than the financial cost? 3. Is it cost-effective for the government to be involved in the institution of the electronic medical record?

Quality of Medical Care

If there were no restrictions on the freedom of health practitioners, there would be a risk that the quality of care might be poor. For example, an unethical doctor might perform unnecessary surgery solely for financial benefit in spite of his knowing that the practice is not for the patient's benefit. There are currently a number of institutions in place that restrict this kind of activity: the requirement for suitable training and credentialing; medico-legal liability; ethical teaching in medical schools and training programs; the natural altruism attending those who enter the health profession; programs within hospitals that self-monitor quality, exert peer pressure, and, sometimes, institute disciplinary action to promote ethical and quality practices; re-credentialing processes; local and national physician groups examining and promulgating the best medical practice for diagnosing and treating certain disorders; hospital committees promoting safety for patients; specialty and subspecialty educational and quality assurance programs; national and international educational meetings; and reputation among doctors, in the community, and on the internet.

Among all of these, the individual physician's desire to perform well is the most important quality control, as it ought to be. Most physicians enter the practice of medicine to assist their patients, which is reinforced by enhanced self-esteem. Physicians realize that every patient interaction can potentially do good. There are few other disciplines that can claim that virtue.

Further, there are significant difficulties in measuring quality. Although randomized, double-blind, controlled therapeutic trials are the gold standard for deciding the best therapy, they are not available in most circumstances. An experienced physician makes the best medical decisions, aware of the clinical circumstances and the medical literature.

Also, the outcome measurement may be found false with time. For example, tight insulin control of type I diabetes mellitus might diminish its complications, but enforced rigid control (through financial incentives to doctors for lower glycosylated hemoglobin levels) might result in more hypoglycemic deaths. Also, the monitoring processes for quality, even with an appropriate measurement, might increase time spent with documentation rather than medical care.

Finally, the physicians' removal from the responsibility of deciding quality care might induce them to function less professionally. Restricting the free expression of the physician as a decision maker can result in a less effective physician. The fundamental question here is whether further curtailment of the physician's liberty, in the name of perceived quality, is worthwhile.

Expansion of Governmental "Entitlement" of Medical Care

The second issue is governmental involvement in the cost of expansion of insurance coverage to the currently uninsured population. Whereas this clearly fulfills the quest for equality of medical care, it comes with a considerable cost. The total monetary cost has not been ascertained yet, but might be along the lines of the cost of Medicare and Medicaid.

Critical to this discussion is the thorny issue of what medical services should be covered with governmental expansion: cosmetic surgery; expensive, recently developed drugs; birth control measures; sexual enhancement drugs; abortion; among many others. How the financial cost is covered will evolve, but would be comprised of the direct cost of care and the diminution of services to patients. Presumably, the cost will be partially offset by a decrease in emergency room and hospital fees for the currently uninsured.

The second cost is to charitable organizations, including religious, community, hospital, freestanding clinics, and doctors' offices, providing free care. These entities will no longer be needed if health insurance becomes universal.

The responsibility for the health of the poor should not only be the government. Health care workers should not be divorced from this responsibility. Further, forced charity funded through taxation, with expansion of this entitlement, is no longer charity. Moving the responsibility of caring for the poor from the health care worker to the government promotes the concept that the health care worker is fundamentally an economic entity. An undesired consequence would be physicians' decisions to limit the number of patients receiving Medicare or Medicaid for economic reasons.

The underlying issue is whether the additional financial costs, which are subsumed by those funding the process through taxation, is acceptable to the country at large, so that equality can be expanded. Are the additional costs balanced by the egalitarian expansion?

Electronic Medical Record

The final issue is whether the institution of the electronic medical record (EMR) for all medical entities (hospitals, clinics, pharmacies, doctors' offices) contains more benefits than detriments (including cost). Most who have practiced medicine realize that the ready retrieval of laboratory results, procedure and surgical reports, patient medications, and summaries of hospitalizations for patients have been significantly beneficial for the practicing physician. Ease in identifying potential drug interactions and patient allergies, with computer-derived warnings, is also achieved, promoting patient safety. The potential for obtaining data on patient outcomes and facilitating research is also enhanced.

However, there are also negative aspects. There are redundancies and unnecessary information contained in the hospitalization EMR. Whereas the major function of the medical record is to transmit cogent information on the patient's health, especially the thoughtful assessments of the attending physician and consulting services, the computer-derived record encourages cutting and pasting without the provision of new information. In addition, unnecessary information is often provided to satisfy the degree of difficulty and time spent with patient interaction to satisfy insurance reimbursement criteria. Finally, the potential for a break in confidentiality of the record is greater, especially with expansion of the availability to other hospital and health services.

On the positive side, further refinement of the system might ameliorate these systematic problems. The cost and negative aspects for establishing and maintaining the EMR should continue to be balanced with its benefits. This continued evaluation should suggest helpful modifications of the EMR, diminishing its negative and increasing its positive values. It has become clear that the EMR, especially in large institutions and hospitals is well-established. Expansion to individual office practices includes other difficulties including the financial cost, the rather user-unfriendly systems available, the additional time spent in its use, and the decreased time in eye-to-eye consultative activity between patient and practitioner.

CONCLUSION

With these three issues there is a reciprocal relationship between the liberty of the medical practitioner and the tax-paying populace and the equalizing efforts of monitoring physician activities beyond current levels, expanding medical insurance to the uninsured population, and generalizing the use of the EMR. As in most legal situations, which are put into place to promote good in the polis, their eventual places will be mediated through resolution of the natural tensions between our unbridled liberty and our moral quest for equality.

This dynamic is highlighted by a single-payer system of health care. In this system, everyone has an equal access to health care (equality is fostered), which is paid through taxation (restriction of liberty to use the money for personal use). It is obvious that there have to be some restrictions or limitations, as the services might exhaust the treasury. Some medical services are not "covered," as they are "too expensive" (restricts liberty for some - those denied treatment, augments it for others - less taxes). Political activation usually mediates the two different points of view.

Since the enactment of the Patient Protection and Affordable Care Act, there has been marked political rancor, as the political fault lines between expansion of equality and costs have widened. The issues raised here remain largely unresolved.

Essay 15. The Legal Preservation of Heterosexual Marriage (53)

Most political mediation balances two aspects of our nature, liberty and the moral quest for some equality (52). The legal framework supporting heterosexual marriage might be adjudicated along this background, as political decisions should be consistent with our nature. Freedom is one of our paramount features, distinguishing us from other life forms and inanimate reality. Counterpoising liberty is our moral sense, which strives to promote some equality to the less fortunate. Often, there is a tension between these two, as the expansion of equality restricts some liberties. This essay is developed along these lines.

It is important to discuss aspects of homosexuality versus heterosexuality from the individual's standpoint. First, what are the criteria for determining whether an individual is a homosexual or a bisexual? During early childhood and adolescence, someone's sexual preference may be ambiguous. Does one homosexual act during the exploratory period of adolescence make someone a homosexual or bisexual by definition? Further, some suggest that the performance of some sexual acts condition future similar sexual acts. Finally, there are many interactions within the same sex that are loving activities, albeit not clearly sexual, including sporting activities, male camaraderie, all-female or all-male functions, female shopping sprees, etc.

As individuals or parents, should our posture be laissez faire, and not encourage or discourage any sexual preference? Are there reasons for each of us to encourage heterosexual over homosexual preference as it naturally leads to fostering biologic families comprised of both genders, which lead to healthful prospering of children? Finally, are there unforeseen consequences for pushing equality too far in this arena, such as choosing roommates in college; participating in same-sex bathrooms, locker room showers and nudity; and simple things such as couple's dances and social clubs? It seems that too much of this expansion might interfere excessively with the freedoms of heterosexuals.

Looked at from the homosexual context, does one want to announce his sexual preference to the world? Shouldn't this be a private concern? Would a male homosexual who has announced his sexuality to everyone suffer disdain if he were to utilize all-male locker rooms? How does this differ from a female who wants to join an all-male locker room? Or a male who wants to join an all-female locker room?

Now, it is important to consider traditional marriage historically to see reasons for its persistence and success. Across different cultures, marriage has promoted protection of the weaker female and children. Unlike many cultures, both currently and historically, Western cultures have been very supportive of females and children. The institution of marriage has been a force that has protected the weaker people from the stronger males, promulgated by our moral nature. Along this line, religious institutions almost universally support traditional marriage. If not currently, then potentially, the diminution of traditional marriage might erode this protective aspect.

These questions are raised without clear-cut answers, but point to potential difficulties with political action. Regardless of how this plays out politically, it should be morally clear that each group should respect the other. One should not unduly criticize or restrict an adult simply on the basis of sexual preference. One can do this without expressing absolute equality.

For example, equality can be fostered among different races without claiming that everyone's skin color is the same. However, trying to be fair to short men by insisting that all basketball players must be less than six feet tall does not make the short man more equal; he is still a short man. Heterosexuals and homosexuals are different. The difficulty is in promoting fairness without eliminating the obvious distinctions.

As a basis for discussion on same-sex marriage being a simple extension of heterosexual marriage, four areas are appropriate: issues of equality or inequality between the two institutions, cultural and religious views on heterosexual marriage, the current legal framework and political reasons for the institution of heterosexual marriage, and concepts of fairness for those who desire to promote equality for both heterosexual and same sex unions.

Clearly, the two institutions are not the same. Most agree that we are an irregular species, with significant differences among us. Whether it is due to genetic or environmental reasons, or a combination of both, some have a sexual preference for the same gender. However, the criterion of sexual preference does not completely explain the distinction of same sex from traditional marriage.

Heterosexual marriage is a culmination of one of our most profound human experiences, the subject of much of our great literature, poetry, music, and religion. The mutual attractiveness that the genders have for one another results in affection and romantic love, leading to submission of the hesitant, less compliant female to the more aggressive male, eventuating in sexual intercourse. Much of our great literature, moral constructs, and religious dicta revolve around this process. A formal or tacit agreement is reached that the male takes responsibility for the smaller and weaker female and the resultant family. Fidelity between the two is mutually accepted. The advantage to the species is the preservation of a structure that enables the healthy development of children. The marriage oaths, in both civil and religious ceremonies, substantiate this institution.

Although same-sex relations can be loving and share mutual fidelity, they are different from conventional marriages, not only in their obviously being of the same gender. They also do not have the same potential for enriching themselves and society with their biologic children. They are more similar in size, strength, and other genetically determined characteristics, and they have different modes of sexual expression.

Secondly, most religious institutions assert the sanctity of heterosexual marriage, and have formalized rules or canons of behavior between the genders, consistent with the formulation expressed above. Moral codes supporting fidelity, modesty, and mutual support are advocated, and these foster healthy family interaction and childhood rearing, beneficial to both society and the individual religions.

Third, most societies and religions have formalized heterosexual marriage legally, which can be viewed as an extension of the individual heterosexual process outlined above. This legal framework does restrict unbridled sexual freedom that could be judged as detrimental, opposing one of the most basic aspects of our nature. However, the legal process supports concepts of financial and societal stability for each partner and for the family, and promotes an environment suitable for the development of children. Particularly, it protects the interests of the weaker women and children from potential harmful effects from the stronger male. Cultures and religions try to foster this protection of the more vulnerable individuals. Most would agree that the legal institutions for heterosexual marriage have had a salutary effect, outweighing the restriction of each partner's freedom. Further, the restriction of this freedom is voluntary, expressing each individual's desire for the restriction.

Finally, turning to same-sex marriage, one can see that concepts of fairness and justice come into play. Is it fair to allow the legal support of heterosexual marriage (including the ability to adopt children; the sharing of employee and union benefits upon the death of one partner; acceptance of each partner as the next of kin to the other; agreement that the marriage is legally binding in all states; and criteria for divorce), but not for same-sex marriage? Clearly there is no restriction of the liberty of those choosing heterosexual marriage through expansion of the legal framework to same-sex marriage. Further, there are distinct societal benefits for expanding this right, as it promotes stable, loving relationships, and expands equality at little expense to liberty. An obvious example of this process might be the curtailment of sexually transmitted disease and the scourge of AIDS.

However, it is important to realize that the legal expansion of marriage to include same-sex marriage does not signal equality with heterosexual marriage. There remain distinct differences outlined above. The cultural, religious, and historical reasons for the legal support of heterosexual marriage are not present in same-sex marriages. In our zest for equality, we should not make a mockery of biologic differences. Further, cultural and religious sensitivities and tenets cannot be ignored. No one should expect that a religious institution should legally be forced to accept same-sex marriage. This would be an unconscionable restriction of religious liberty.

In addition, there may be unintended consequences from laws attempting to assert that the unions are the same. Do homosexuals want to risk hostility between them and religious institutions that bar homosexual marriage? Might there be constitutional issues with religious freedom? Does the presence of same-sex marriage pit itself against conventional marriage in private social functions? Does the type of marriage have any role in adoption agencies' determination of the best set of parents for a child? Do homosexuals want to engage in this contest? Finally, there are privacy issues that might be abridged and become detrimental to those who wish to keep their sexual preference private.

If same-sex unions are provided the rights of heterosexual marriage, why do those advocates want to equate the two unions when they are obviously different? Is it to promote the freedom of same-sex unions or to restrict the freedom of those engaged in heterosexual marriage? Doesn't the political identity of the two unions negate the original designation with all of its cultural, religious, and moral teaching?

Homosexual couples may find that pushing this too far may be counterproductive, producing animosity and resentment. Same-sex couples desire respect for their union, but respect cannot be legislated. Respect is earned. For example, bath houses for homosexual men promoted promiscuity, sexually transmitted diseases, and AIDS in the 1980s and 1990s. Laws eschewing this practice, advocated by the male homosexual community, would advance the respect for homosexual coupling. This practice could be compared to responsible heterosexuals who condemn and try to restrict prostitution. Respect for same-sex unions will come with their establishing their own traditions, showing benefits to those within its traditions and society at large, as societies have done with traditional marriages. Feelings, sentiments, religious canons, and traditional beliefs cannot be legislated away. In the same sense, same-sex couples should respect their parents' unions and their traditions, established over the millennia, one of the special features of human dignity.

In conclusion, heterosexual and same-sex marriages have distinct differences but share many values. The legal expansion to include same-sex unions clearly benefits a segment of our population without infringing upon the rights of supporters of traditional marriage. Perhaps each marriage should have a modifier, either traditional or same-sex. Alternatively, civil unions could be expanded such that there are little significant legal preferences for traditional marriage over civil unions. Presumably some specific legal judgments will be necessary for each entity. For example, homosexual domestic partners might not want to announce their sexuality formally, but they may wish to obtain the right for the partner to share in his employer's health benefits. Finally, the religious and cultural sensitivities supporting traditional marriage should not suffer any legal repercussions from this expansion. Nor should supporters of one type deprecate the other.

Essay 16. Diet, Obesity, and Political Involvement (54)

Introduction

This essay provides information on nutrition, diet, nutritional science, and obesity to serve as a reference in teaching patients these issues. It is composed by a gastroenterologist who has been engaged in clinical gastroenterology and nutrition, research, and teaching in an academic medical center for 35 years. It also relates the information to conclusions on reasonable involvement of the national government in these topics. Its audience might also include the interested, well-educated, lay public. Hence, excessive scientific parlance and referencing have been avoided.

Any governmental program that mandates certain dietary prescriptions or proscriptions is a restriction of liberty, so that the general good can be advanced, in a quest to provide some beneficial equality. The diminished freedom is evident by a decreased availability of some goods or the implementation of a tax to support the program. Therefore the reasons should be compelling to justify the restrictions. The author is an Emeritus Professor at a major medical institution. He has practiced clinical medicine for 38 years, served as division chief of gastroenterology for 12 years and was chief of nutritional support for 30 years. Examples of nutritional issues are given to clarify the author's point of view and to facilitate the understanding of recommendations given in the concluding section.

Robert M. Craig, M.D.

Background

Obesity is a major health problem for developed countries, and has recently been identified more frequently in children. It contributes to type 2 diabetes mellitus, arteriosclerosis (including stroke and coronary artery disease), musculoskeletal disorders, and some cancers. It is also a component of the metabolic syndrome comprised of obesity, elevated plasma lipids, arteriosclerosis, type 2 diabetes mellitus, and fatty liver disease. Further, it contributes to diminished mobility in the elderly and in those with musculoskeletal problems. Finally, it is a contributing factor in postoperative morbidity and mortality.

Consequently, there have been many measures advocated to address the problem, including specific diets, exercise programs, dietary medications, and vitamins. There has also been increasing attention to measures to alter the dietary habits in children and teenagers. Even surgical treatment of the morbidly obese has been employed. In spite of these efforts, there has been little impact on the problem. Specific diets have also been advocated to promote general "good health," often with little scientific credence or well-documented value demonstrated.

Before developing a set of recommendations that would be useful to address these issues, it is necessary to discuss the nature, physiology, and biochemistry of humans; an understanding of how we ingest and absorb nutrients; our ability to use nutrients to warm our bodies and permit locomotion; the results from excess assimilated fuel and the meaning of energy balance; the basic food stuffs that we ingest, and for what each is required; and how we are related to other animals in our physiology and biochemistry. Along these lines, concepts of adaptability and interchange among the nutrients will be discussed. Finally, discussions of micronutrients, the scientific method to explore efficacy, some nutritional fallacies, and recommendations will be presented.

Nutrient Absorption and Adaptability

Carbohydrates, proteins, and fats have to undergo digestion of the large molecules into small entities to permit passage through the intestinal lining cells into the blood stream. Enzymes are proteins present on the lining of the intestine or secreted into the gut lumen to promote digestion. Fats are converted into fatty acids and glycerol, proteins into amino acids or small combinations of amino acids (peptides), and long chain carbohydrates into smaller carbohydrates (such as starch into glucose). The smaller molecules pass through the intestinal wall more easily and are often facilitated in this passage by carrier mechanisms present on the gut membrane.

The digestive process is extremely efficient. Under normal circumstances, almost all of the ingested carbohydrate and protein and 95% of the fat are absorbed. There is significant adaptability of the enzymatic and carrier mechanisms to changes in the ingestion of nutrients. For example, the enzyme responsible for splitting lactose, the sugar in milk, into glucose and galactose, is "down-regulated," and is in lower concentration, when less lactose (milk) is ingested. This allows for protein synthesis elsewhere. On the other hand, iron absorption is facilitated across the intestinal membrane when there is too little iron in the blood. The intestine, then, compensates for variations in nutrient intake. In addition, the avid absorption of most carbohydrates makes some of the claims that certain carbohydrates (starch) are preferred to its constituents (glucose) incredible. Measured blood glucose is identical following the ingestion of an equivalent weight of glucose or starch.

Nutrients and Their Metabolic Handling

An understanding of the categories of nutrients is necessary to grasp concepts of energy balance and obesity. Humans evolved from creatures of the sea, necessitating water and the major minerals, sodium (Na) and chloride (Cl). In a sense, seawater has been transported into our blood and tissue fluids. The cells of our tissues require the other mineral macronutrients: potassium, bicarbonate, magnesium, calcium, and phosphate. There are finely tuned mechanisms involving the gastro-intestinal tract, the kidneys, the blood, the tissues, and the membranes of cells, assuring homeostasis. These macronutrients do not contribute to energy balance or obesity, but they are required for survival.

The three nutrients contributing to energy balance are proteins, carbo-hydrates, and lipids (fats). Proteins are comprised of strings of constitu-ent amino acids. Following digestion, the amino acids are transported into the blood stream and body organs, especially the liver, for new protein synthesis. These synthesized proteins provide for our bodies' structure in cells, tissues, and organs; enzymes; hormones; and other circulating messengers. All of our bodily functions are dependent upon proteins.

Carbohydrates and lipids provide energy for the functioning of the body, including maintenance of heat, movement, and the cellular chemical processes involved in homeostasis. Although there are some dietary carbohydrates and fats that are "essential," and cannot be syn-thesized from other nutrients, there is interchangeability among them. The constituents of carbohydrates and lipids enter various intermediary metabolic processes, mostly in the liver, that allow for this interchange and synthesis of new molecules. The metabolism of the constituents of carbohydrates and lipids generates energy for the above-enumerated functions. Excessive ingestion leads to storage as fat.

Digested proteins also enter the intermediary metabolic cycles as their constituent amino acids and can produce energy or be synthesized into carbohydrates (gluconeogenesis) or fats. Excess proteins are, then, stored as fat. These three moieties have specialized uses, their essential functions, which cannot be performed by the other two, but they are exchangeable from the standpoint of energy production and fat storage.

However, the amounts of energy generation from the three are not identical. The measurement used for this is the calorie which is the amount of heat required to raise the temperature of one gram of water one degree centigrade, usually expressed in kilocalories (kcals) or capitalized, Calories (Cals). 1000 calories equals 1 kcal. The oxidation ("burning") of fats produce about nine kcals per gram; proteins and carbohydrates somewhat less than four. Therefore fats are much more energy dense than the other two. One can see that eating an amount (weight) of fats will allow for over twice the energy production from an equivalent amount of carbohydrates and protein. In addition, ingestion of fat promotes much more fat storage, when excessive, than equivalent amounts of proteins or carbohydrates.

The interchange among these three nutrients by means of cyclical metabolic mechanisms should not surprise us, as nature is replete with cyclical processes, such as the CO_2, issued from the respiration of plants and animals, used in the photosynthetic production of carbohydrates and oxygen by chlorophyll-containing plants. The interdependence of plants and animals is evident in this cycle. Another example of a cyclical process is the CO_2-calcium carbonate cycle in the ocean and land, important in climatology theory. The interchangeability of our three basic food substances allows for thriving humans in polar regions, which might have 90% of their calories provided by fats (polar bear or seal meat and blubber), and many Asians with 90% of their calories, carbohydrate (rice).

Many of the metabolic processes in human cells are also contained in all or most animals. Our earth has undergone many changes that have required adaptable metabolic machinery, and redundant metabolic processes to assist in dealing with the changes. Life is the most enduring characteristic of Earth, expressed by living cells, which have enormous capacity to survive in varied environments, through evolutionary change and adaptability.

The need to store metabolic fuel is determined by the metabolic rate of the organism. If fuel intake exceeds output, storage of fat eventuates. The metabolic rate is comprised of the basal energy expenditure (basal metabolic rate, or BMR) and the energy required for any additional physical work. The BMR assures maintenance of our body heat and all of the physical processes involved in life. One can see that the amount of calories consumed increase with exercise. Conversely, the amount stored as fat is increased with less exercise.

The Influence of Genetics, Hormones, and the Hypothalamus in Weight Control

There is mounting evidence that there are significant genetic determinants of obesity. In our daily observations we can see this relationship. We are a varied and unequal species in many respects, including our body habitus. Although eating rituals may be established through acculturation, it is striking how much parents and their children resemble each other in physical appearance. Further, observations of eating habits of individuals who are obese compared to those who tend to be thin usually show that the obese are much more careful in selecting what and how much they eat than the thin. The thin seem to be able to maintain thinness without involving any conscious control.

These homely notions are also supported scientifically. In the 1960s, a trial of overfeeding prison inmates showed that their metabolism sped up during overfeeding, and allowed for rapid weight loss with the return to a regular diet (55). On the other hand, those overfed who were prone to obesity did not shed their weight as easily with dietary restitution. In addition, biologically identical twin studies show that the tendency to obesity persists in both twins, regardless whether they are brought up in the same or different households (56, 57). Recently, these concepts have received more credence in studies implicating a satiety hormonal factor, leptin; a hunger-stimulating hormone, ghrelin; and the hypothalamus (55). The upshot of all of these investigations is that obesity may not be under as much conscious control as was originally thought. This is not to say that it is not under conscious control. It is to stress that those tending to obesity would have to involve more conscious control than those genetically tending to be thin.

Micronutrients and the Recommended Dietary Allowance (RDA)

The micronutrients are vitamins and minerals that are required for optimal expression of life, but are found in relatively small quantities in the body. Excessive ingestion of micronutrients can be stored or excreted from the body. Fat-soluble vitamins, including vitamins A and D, are stored in the liver and can produce harm in excessive amounts. Water-soluble vitamins, such as vitamin C and the B vitamins, are generally harmless, even when ingested in large quantities, as the excess is excreted in the urine. However these water-soluble vitamins, especially pyridoxine, can occasionally be detrimental, particularly when used chronically in high amounts or when associated with kidney failure. Obvious examples of harmful, mineral micronutrients when ingested excessively include iron, copper and manganese. Calcium, magnesium, potassium, chloride, and sodium are macronutrient minerals, as they are abundant in the body.

A daunting task has been the development of recommended dietary allowances (RDAs) for micronutrients. This is the amount that prevents a deficiency disease for each nutrient. The difficulties in making the determination can be illustrated by the example of scurvy. British sailors in the seventeenth and eighteenth centuries developed bleeding gums and skin lesions, ascribed to diminished intake of vitamin C. They were eventually called limeys as the provision of limes, which have an abundance of vitamin C, prevented the development of scurvy when supplied on the ocean-going ships. One can see the difficulties involved in determining the amount of vitamin C needed to prevent or treat the disease, and translate this into the amount of limes to ingest daily. Ideally, those affected with scurvy could enter a trial involving various daily amounts of vitamin C, and find out the least amount needed to rectify the problem. Of course, a suitable measurement, such as a bleeding time or a measurement of blood vitamin C, would be necessary to make the judgment objective. Finally, the amount of vitamin C contained in each lime would allow calculation of how much of the RDA is contained in each lime. This calculation would have to take into account the freshness of the limes, as the amount of vitamin C would probably be higher in the fresher limes. From an ethical standpoint, the trial could not be done, as it would be inappropriate to give the scorbutic individuals the low doses of vitamin C.

Similar problems arise in determining the RDA for all micronutrients. One approach to this has used blood levels for a micronutrient, relating this to some effect on the body. One can screen a large, healthy, population and find the average and variance of the micronutrient, then compare this to a group that has some defect, presumably due to a diminished store of the micronutrient. Then a difficult translation to the amount of the micronutrient required to promote restitution of the blood level would be required.

The body has exquisitely controlled mechanisms for the absorption and excretion of nutrients, such as the efficient excretion of excess (Na) and water-soluble vitamins; and the variable absorption of iron (Fe), dependent upon bodily stores of Fe. There may be similar control mechanisms involving all of the micronutrients. Further, most plant and animal cells that we ingest contain micronutrients, although in variable amounts, allowing for micronutrient assimilation from most things that we eat. It is noteworthy that a baby can live on milk alone for over a year. Presumably, humans could live on eggs alone, which might contain all of the necessary micronutrients.

Special Nutritional Problems, Gluten, Food Allergy, Food Intolerance, Aspartame

Gluten is a general term for some of the proteins found in wheat, barley, and rye, and is responsible for celiac disease (CD), a relatively common malady, affecting around 1% of those of northern European ancestry, and present worldwide at a lower incidence. Although its most common presentations currently are iron deficiency or non-specific gastrointestinal complaints, it can present with neurological symptoms, severe diarrhea, weight loss, nutritional deficiencies, menstrual irregularity and infertility, liver abnormalities, and a skin disorder. It is diagnosed by blood studies and by biopsy of the intestinal epithelium and is cured by the observance of a diet that avoids gluten.

Our most common gastrointestinal disturbance is irritable bowel syndrome (IBS), which may have the same symptoms as celiac disease. However, most patients with IBS do not have celiac disease. Current investigations are underway to see if a subgroup of IBS patients is intolerant to gluten-containing diets, without having CD. This information has been expanded by many who have promulgated avoidance of gluten for a host of different symptoms with little or no evidence supporting the contentions. Studies of symptom relief from dietary gluten withdrawal in IBS is much more difficult to accomplish successfully when compared to studies in CD. In CD there are specific markers that can be measured objectively. Further, CD is potentially life threatening, making the incentive to accomplish the study higher than in a similar study on IBS patients. Although IBS may be responsible for many symptoms, its improvement cannot be gauged easily by objective measurements, and it does not pose a risk of death. When compared to our paradigmatic example of limes, vitamin C, and scurvy, one can realize that a reliable study of gluten withdrawal in IBS would be much more difficult to accomplish.

There are food intolerances in normal individuals, often more prominent in those with IBS. Many of these are idiosyncratic, and do not lend themselves to general therapeutic dicta. Although food allergy has been suggested as being responsible for these intolerances, classic allergic mechanisms, presenting clinically with a skin rash or trouble breathing, are relatively uncommon.

It is not uncommon to read in the lay literature concerns about the use of aspartame, an artificial sweetener, much sweeter per amount than glucose, fructose, or sucrose. Some have claimed that allowing too much sweeteners in children has promoted excessive consumption of sweet foods to the exclusion of other more "nutritionally replete" foods. The scientific evaluation of this proposal is discussed in the following section, but it should be stressed that aspartame is comprised of a di-peptide of two amino acids, aspartic acid and phenylalanine, which are found in most proteins. It is nearly completely digested into its compo-nent amino acids, although a small amount is absorbed as the dipeptide. There might be rare intolerances to the dipeptide, but the constituent amino acids are as safe as those present in all the proteins that we eat (an exception is excessive phenylalanine ingestion in patients with the rare congenital illness, phenylketonuria (PKU), as phenylalanine is one of the two amino acids in aspartame).

Scientific Evaluation and Controlled Studies

If one wants to do a trial to see if an intervention is therapeutically use-ful for a disease, the best type of investigation is a randomized, doubly blind trial. That is one in which members of a population receive the questioned therapy or a placebo on a randomized basis, and neither the patient nor the treating and evaluating health workers know which treatment is given. If the chosen endpoint shows improvement in the condition in the group receiving the therapy vs. the placebo, then the therapy is considered of value. In the scurvy example, if a trial of vita-min C is shown to cure scurvy when compared to placebo, the vitamin C is considered therapeutic. Things are more complicated with studies involving limes, as it would be difficult to get a lime placebo.

Some studies of specific nutrients have been performed to see if the nutrient has a salutary role. Experimental studies have suggested that vitamins with anti-oxidant properties, such as vitamin A or vitamin E, might have a binding effect on free radicals, or reactive oxygen species, and might prevent or reverse cancer. Unfortunately, well controlled randomized, double-blind studies have not shown efficacy. For example, a Scandinavian study of cigarette smokers did not show a reduction in the incidence of lung cancer in those given vitamins A and E (58).

In more complex problems, such as obesity, one can see other confounding influences. In a trial of a high fat- vs. a low fat-containing diet, various things need to be "controlled" to exclude their influence: the other components of the diets, for example protein content, should be equivalent; there has to be assurance that the diets are rigorously followed; a decision has to be made whether to keep the caloric content the same or to allow the subject to eat as much as he wants of the diet; the amount of physical exercise must be the same for each group; the two groups must be as close to identical as possible, usually achieved statistically by randomization; and the duration of the study should be long enough to achieve meaningful results. Many of these characteristics cannot be achieved in the outpatient setting, and, yet, it is outpatients who will be taking the advice derived from the studies. Most weight loss studies comparing various diets have not controlled for calories and have shown efficacy in the short term, but not the long term. This should not surprise us, as weight loss or gain is related to total calories ingested, not to the type of food (fat, carbohydrate or protein), due to the caloric interchangeability of these nutrients; and to the amount of physical exercise performed.

An example may clarify this issue. A popular diet along these lines is the DASH (Dietary Approaches to Stop Hypertension) eating plan (59). This diet contains foods with less sodium chloride, calories, and cholesterol than that of the usual American diet. In addition, an exercise program is included and encouraged. The balance among fats, carbohydrates, and fats is similar to that of the American diet. One can see the difficulties in doing a study to substantiate that the diet is an improvement over other diets for prolonged weight loss. One would have to control for salt intake, exercise, and caloric input, and the study would have to be sufficiently long to show prolonged efficacy. We already know that exercise and caloric restriction promote weight loss; what has not been demonstrated is efficacy of one diet over another. The difficulty in achieving prolonged weight loss in the long term is due to the challenge of prolonged caloric restriction.

As mentioned above, some have advocated avoidance of sweet foods in children as they might condition children to eat less "nutritionally rich" foods. Note that exclusion of fruits is not included in the proscription, even though many are quite sweet. One can see the difficulties in doing a well-controlled study of this thesis, randomizing one group of children to have no artificial sweeteners and no sweetened beverages (except "natural" fruit juices), the other with no restrictions, for a prolonged duration, perhaps a year, and measuring the effect on body-mass-index (a measurement of body fat content). The most important chore would be the exclusion of sweetened beverages in our society and the onerous task of supervising the restrictions. Those of us with children and grandchildren understand the difficulties.

Recommendations for Governmental Involvement in Diet and Nutrition

1. Diets for obesity prevention. The body has many mechanisms in place that allow for varying absorption, synthesis, interconversion, elimination and retention of nutrients to augment survival under varying circumstances. It should not be surprising that specific diets to control, modify, or prevent obesity have not shown efficacy over simple caloric restriction, fulfilling scientific scrutiny. Since the amounts of micro and macronutrients are present in variable amounts among foods, the recommendation that diets should strive to achieve some balance is reasonable. A mother nagging her youngsters to "eat their vegetables"

sounds like good teaching. Individual food tastes determine much of what we eat, and our tastes vary widely, both among different cultures and as each of us goes through life's stages. Gustatory satisfaction is one of the pleasures of life, and many of our social engagements take place around food and liquid consumption. Programs to modify this behavior will usually fail, especially long term. Therefore, governmental programs trying to force dietary changes, when there is no strong, scientific evidence supporting the measures, is an unwise restriction of liberty, by limiting the freedom to choose different foods and by the cost for its implementation (a type of tax, which is a diminution of the freedom to use the money elsewhere).

2. Obesity should be considered a characteristic, similar to other differences among members of our species (height, skin color, eye color, intelligence, sociability, etc.) and should not be an object of scornful criticism. Children chiding the obese child are similar to other bullying practices, which parents and other adults should abjure. The obese individual is prone to be obese. He is not responsible for the tendency to obesity. Weight control for the obese remains one of the major challenges during their lives. A thin person who does not have to be careful about what he eats should not be applauded for his thinness. Rather the obese person who is able to control his weight through caloric limitation and exercise should be recognized for his noble achievement.

3. The most effective strategy for weight control is to affect change on the other side of the metabolic equation, exercise. Weight gain is directly related to caloric input and inversely related to metabolic activity and exercise. It is unusual to see an obese tennis professional or lumberjack. Exercise should be encouraged in all of us for weight control and general fitness. It would seem reasonable to have governmental influence on exercise in children, with mandatory gym and recess activities.

4. Food labeling for specific purposes. It is also reasonable for governmental involvement in labeling contents of food that would specify harmful ingredients for specific diseases, such as gluten for celiac

disease and phenylalanine for phenylketonuria. In addition, it is reasonable to indicate the caloric content of foods, as the information might influence one's behavior in weight control programs. Further, listing Na and K content of foods might assist consumers with heart and kidney disorders. The cost involved in labeling all of the micronutrients for each food item, both for the manufacturer and the monitoring, and, eventually, to the consumer seems excessive. The guidepost should be whether the labeling of a nutrient content is of proven use in preventing or ameliorating disease.

5. Governmental labeling of "nutritious foods," vs. "non-nutritious foods" is not well supported by well-performed, scientific, studies. This should be eschewed, along with labeling sweet foods, those containing fats, or artificial sweeteners, except for aspartame in those with PKU. Further, governmental involvement in the amount of Na, fats, sugars, starch, etc. that is "healthy" should not be advocated. No food is intrinsically "unhealthy" for the general population, but its healthiness is dependent upon a point of view. For example, someone subject to heart failure or with failing kidneys might require salt restriction (Na), whereas Na restriction for the general population might be harmful. Listing some carbohydrates as "healthy" (those in fruit juices) whereas others (fructose in cola products) as "unhealthy," does not make sense as each carbohydrate eventuates in the same metabolic cycles within the liver, and are metabolically interchangeable.

6. The FDA does a responsible assessment of drugs, and should be the judge of the safety of artificial sweeteners. Aspartame has been studied quite exhaustively and is deemed safe by the FDA, which should be the final arbiter. Any new sweeteners should be subjected to the same scrutiny, and any ongoing information on sweeteners should be within the province of the FDA. Claims for excessive use of vitamins, so-called megavitamin therapy, should be evaluated similarly to any drug product assessment, including evidence of risks. In general the RDA listed for vitamins, determined by FDA evaluation, and included in multivitamins, is a reasonable guideline for general use. Specialized

considerations, such as additional folic acid during pregnancy, or increased vitamin D intake in those shown to be deficient, should be encouraged.

7. Various dietary programs should undergo the same scientific evaluation that other treatment programs undergo. Clearly, it is unjustified for governmental advocation of one dietary program over another, when there are no hard data. Simple measures to limit caloric intake, regardless of the source, should be the mainstay. For reasons specified above; including adaptability, interchangeability among nutrients, and cultural and genetic predispositions; it is unlikely that one specific dietary program will prove useful for weight control over another for the general population.

FOOTNOTES AND REFERENCES

1. Craig RM. The Good Life and other Philosophical Essays on Human Nature. Yorkshire Publishing, Oklahoma (2014)

2. Some of the imagery was suggested to me when I read Henri Bergson's Creative Energy. After I completed the original version of this essay, I read Arthur Hermann's book, The Cave and the Light, Random House (2013), where he discussed Bergson. Hermann's large book is on the effect of Aristotle and Plato throughout history.

3. Penrose R, Fashion, Faith, and Fantasy in the Physics of the Universe. Princeton University Press (2016). This book is a thorough review of the current state of affairs of quantum theory and general relativity theory. It is a difficult read, especially for those who do not have a mathematical background, but it is worth the effort.

4. Nagel E and Newman JR. Gödel's Proof. Rutledge Classics, London (1958).

5. Wignall, PB. The Worst of Times. Princeton University Press, Princeton, New Jersey (2015).

6. Boyd JM, Drevland RM, Downs, et al. Archaeal ApbC/Npb35 homologs function as iron-sulfate cluster carrier proteins. Journal Bacteriology 191:1490-1497 (2009).

7. Lane N. The vital question. WW Norton and Co. New York (2015). Lane argues persuasively that the earliest life forms may have started within inorganic protocells in the walls of alkaline vents in the oceans

about 4 billion years ago. The alkaline effluent bathed the walls of the vents, setting up an electrical potential difference with the slightly acidic ocean. The potential difference was harnessed as an energy source for the generation of primitive molecules.

8. McFadden J and Al-Khalil. Life on the Edge. Crown Publishers, New York (2014).

9. For those more interested in the chemical process of oxidation and reduction in living entities, I suggest references 6-8, which discuss the thermodynamics and chemistry of oxidation and reduction in more detail. I also offer the following: Most of the chemical reactions that occur with life are oxidation/reduction reactions. With reduction, an atom receives an electron or donates a proton and is reduced. Oxidation is the converse, as an atom donates an electron or receives a proton and is oxidized. In the Fe/S rich milieu of Earth's early history, Ferrous ($Fe+2$) donates an electron and becomes oxidized ($Fe+3$) and, in the process, harnesses energy. With photosynthesis, under the influence of the sun's energetic photon, the oxygen atom of water is oxidized to O_2 by donating an electron to the carbon atom of carbon dioxide (CO_2). The carbon atom is reduced to methane (CH_4) or another hydrocarbon and is energized. There are intermediary chemical reactions in the chloroplast that function as an "electron train" that deliver the electron to the carbon atom of CO_2. The chemical formula for the process is $2H_2O + CO_2 = 2O_2 + CH_4$. In words, two molecules of water combine with one molecule of carbon dioxide producing 2 molecules of oxygen (oxidized) and one molecule of methane (reduced). The reverse of photosynthesis is respiration or oxidation of the energy source. The methane (or other hydrocarbon) is oxidized by oxygen to carbon dioxide. Respiration (oxidation) is present in all living things, although it does not always involve oxygen (as in the Fe example). Photosynthesis is present only in green plants.

10. Quantum mechanical theory states that a particle demonstrates both particulate and wave functions. The uncertainty principle indicates that

the wave function aspect (being able to be in multiple places at once, only describable statistically) collapses when its location is described or "measured."

11. The interested reader might study reference 7, which contains electron micrographs of the various intracellular organelles: mitochondria, ribosomes, nuclei, chromosomes, and the membranous structures. Briefly, the chromosomes contain DNA, which has formulas for protein synthesis, written in its own language of purines and pyrimidines. Messenger RNA obtains the blueprint from DNA, and delivers it to ribosomal RNA, which have short segments of RNA containing amino acids for protein synthesis. The synthesis of the proteins from the designated amino acids occurs in the endoplasmic reticulum, instructed by the DNA and mediated by messenger RNA, ribosomal RNA, and its attached amino acids.

12. A thorough treatment of African slavery documents these statements, in Lovejoy, Paul E: Transformations in Slavery. A History of Slavery in Africa. Third Edition. New York: Cambridge University Press (2012).

13. A discussion of black African slavery in the United States can be found in Baptist, Edward E. The Half has never been Told. Slavery and the Making of American Capitalism. New York: Basic Books (2014).

14. Ibid, Lovejoy, Paul E. This historical development is covered well in his latter chapters.

15. Ibid, Baptist, Edward E. The events leading up to the Civil War are discussed.

16. Mitchell, Margaret. Gone With the Wind. New York: The Macmillan Company (1936).

17. Stowe, Harriet Beecher. Uncle Tom's Cabin. New York: Barnes and Noble (1853).

18. Leo Tolstoy. War and Peace.

19. Ibid, Baptist, Edward E. Torture during the period of southern slavery and its effect on productivity of slaves is documented.

20. Ibid, Lovejoy, Paul E. The dates for the gradual dissolution of worldwide slavery are provided.

21. Acemoglu, Daron and Robinson, James A. Why Nations Fail. New York: Crown Publishing (2012). The concepts of extractive and inclusive states and how these influence the economic success of a nation are discussed.

22. Hazen P. The story of Earth. New York. Viking-Penguin Publishers (2012).

23. Harari YN. Sapiens. A brief history of humankind. Harper Collins, New York (2015).

24. Hublin J-J, et al. New fossils from Jebel Irhoud, Morocco and the pan-African origin of Homo sapiens. Nature 546: 289-292 (2017)

25. Koven S. Letter to a Young Female Physician. New Engl J Med. 376: 1907-9 (2017)

26. William James. Writings 1902-1910. Ed Bruce Kuklick. Literary Classics of the United States. New York (1987). This extensive volume of his lectures displays his ability to speak philosophically on some metaphysical concepts. His lectures on pragmatism and a pluralistic universe are fitting. (pp 479-820).

27. The Everly Brothers were popular singers from the mid twentieth century who sang the song, Dream.

28. C. S. Lewis was a prominent mid-twentieth century theologian and philosopher.

29. Alfred Lord Tennyson's poem, "Break, break, break."

30. Bergson, H. Creative Evolution.

31. Gleick J. Chaos. Making a New Science. Penguin group (1987). This remarkable book describes this new science clearly, showing the difficulties classical science has in explaining chaotic behavior. For example, the "butterfly effect" describes far reaching effects from a distant, fluttering butterfly.

32. Ludwig Wittgenstein was a prominent philosopher of the 20th century. He felt that the main role of the philosopher was to analyze propositions carefully, as many can be clarified through the analysis of language. He was a fore-runner of the Logical Positivist school of philosophy, which shared many of his philosophical ideas. According to him, many of the ideas discussed in this volume are not appropriate for philosophical inquiry. To the contrary, I believe all of the ideas expressed here are appropriate to philosophy.

33. William Shakespeare. Romeo and Juliet.

34. J. P. Sartre was a prominent twentieth century philosopher, often considered the most influential thinker in the Existential school of philosophy. His most prodigious work was Being and Nothingness, in which he explored aspects of human consciousness. For him consciousness or "self" had three components, the entire panoply of everything someone has done and stands for (In Itself), how one is perceived by others (For Others), and that which someone makes of himself (For Itself).

35. C. S. Lewis was a well known, twentieth century Christian theologian and philosopher who frequently explored the complexities of morality, stressing the importance of what the person is experiencing in his heart and mind. One must know all of the aspects of someone's action when exploring the morality of the event, the "entire story."

36. Gustav Flaubert's famous, nineteenth century, French novel, Madame Bovary, portrayed a woman enthralled with the concept of romantic, sexual love, and proceeded to act out her fantasies with multiple sexual affairs, having no concern for the consequences to her husband, child or decency. Boris Pasternak's twentieth century, Russian novel, Dr. Zhivago, portrayed a physician and poet during and after World War I and the Russian Revolution, who became involved with another woman during his long absence from his wife during and after the war.

37. W. B. Yeats' poem, Crazy Jane talks with the Bishop.

38. Clarence Thomas was eventually confirmed as a United States Supreme Court justice. There was acrimonious debate concerning a charge of sexual harassment by one of his female coworkers.

39. Jonathan Haidt, The Righteous Mind, Pantheon Books, New York (2012). This scholarly, insightful, often humorous, book was a delight to read. Anyone interested in the nature of morality would benefit from its reading. I can relate to this story, as I have been guilty of similar behavior. As an excuse, it is easy to become embroiled, selfishly, in one's own activities, to the exclusion of others' interests. This is an excuse, not a justification of the action or inaction. Further, lying about the inaction compounds the immorality. Humans have a tremendous capacity to behave badly.

40. Martin Heidegger was a prominent twentieth century philosopher whose major intellectual emphasis was ontological. He explored the nature of being, especially the being of humans. Some of his descriptions

of being in his proclaimed book, Being and Time, are poetic and invoke religious feeling.

41. The American Heritage Dictionary of the English Language. Houghton, Mifflin, Harcourt. Boston (2011).

42. During the interrogation of President Clinton on his involvement with a young lady on his staff, he made this famous claim.

43. The mind-body problem is also discussed in essay 1, Human Nature.

44. This essay was presented orally at the Chicago Literary Club and was published in its compendium.

45. This essay is an updated modification of my original essay published in The Good Life and Other Philosophical Essays on Human Nature, Yorkshire Publishing (2014). The discussions expressed here remain relevant.

46. Ward, P. D. and D. Brownlee. The Life and Death of Planet Earth. New York: Times Books (2012). This is a very readable book, containing detailed geological, chemical, and astronomical information.

47. Wignall, P. B. The Worst of Times. Princeton, New Jersey: Princeton University Press (2015). This book describes and explains the mass extinctions occurring during the time of the super-continent, Pangea.

48. Blunder, J. and Arndt, A. S, Eds., State of the climate in 2016. Bull Amer Meteor Soc Si-S245 (2017)

49. Diamond, Jarrod. Collapse. New York: Penguin Group (2011). This is a thoughtful book that addresses the environmental issues that we face.

50. D. Acemoglu and Robinson J. A. Why Nations Fail. New York:Crown Publishing Group (2012).

51. This is an update of my original essay on this subject, published in The Good Life and Other Philosophical Essays on Human Nature, Yorkshire Publishing, Oklahoma (2014). Most of the issues raised in the essay remain unresolved.

52. A more thorough discussion of our nature and its relationship to political involvement is found in essay 1, Human Nature, and essay 9, The Good Life, in this volume.

53. This essay is modified since the United States Supreme Court judged that marriage between homosexuals is a constitutional right. The essay first appeared in my book, The Good Life and Other Essays on Human Nature, Yorkshire Publishing, Oklahoma (2014). Most of the considerations remain current, especially those related to religious freedom, freedom of association, and respect for others' differences.

54. This essay is a slightly modified version of my editorial published in the Journal of Clinical Gastroenterology 49:633-7 (2015).

55. Jou C, The biology and genetics of obesity-a century of inquiries. N Engl J Med 370:1874-7 (2014).

56. Stunkard AJ, Sorenson TIA, Harris C. An adoption study of human obesity. N Engl J Med 314:193-8 (1986).

57. Stunkard AJ, Harris JR, Pedersen NL, McClearn GE. The body mass index of twins who have been reared apart. N Engl J Med 322:1483-7 (1990).

58. The Alpha-tocopherol Beta Carotene Cancer Prevention Study Group. The effect of vitamin E and beta carotene on the incidence of

lung cancer and other cancers in male smokers. N Engl J Med 330:1029-35 (1994).

59. Dietary Approaches to Stop Hypertension. National Institutes of Health Publication No. 06-4082, April 2006

CPSIA information can be obtained
at www.ICGtesting.com
Printed in the USA
FSOW04n1603151217
41930FS